FREE DVD ... FREE ... FREE DVD

Certified Diabetes Educator Exam Essential Test Tips DVD from Trivium Test Prep!

Dear Customer,

Thank you for purchasing from Trivium Test Prep! We're honored to help you prepare for your Certified Diabetes Educator Exam.

To show our appreciation, we're offering a **FREE *Certified Diabetes Educator Exam Essential Test Tips* DVD by Trivium Test Prep**. Our DVD includes 35 test preparation strategies that will make you successful on the Certified Diabetes Educator Exam. All we ask is that you email us your feedback and describe your experience with our product. Amazing, awful, or just so-so: we want to hear what you have to say!

To receive your **FREE *Certified Diabetes Educator Exam Essential Test Tips* DVD**, please email us at 5star@triviumtestprep.com. Include "Free 5 Star" in the subject line and the following information in your email:

1. The title of the product you purchased.
2. Your rating from 1 – 5 (with 5 being the best).
3. Your feedback about the product, including how our materials helped you meet your goals and ways in which we can improve our products.
4. Your full name and shipping address so we can send your FREE *Certified Diabetes Educator Exam Essential Test Tips* DVD.

If you have any questions or concerns please feel free to contact us directly at 5star@triviumtestprep.com. Thank you!

- Trivium Test Prep Team

TABLE OF CONTENTS

I. ASSESSMENT OF LEARNING

The Phases of the Teaching and Learning Process - - 7

Motivation, Readiness to Learn and Behavior Change - 17

Assessing Developmental Status - - - - 33

II. ASSESSMENT OF STATUS

Collecting Health History Data - - - - 41

Assessing Medication Regimens - - - - 47

Assessing Support Systems and Consumption Habits - 53

Assessing Psychosocial and Mental Health - - - 57

Assessing Barriers to Self-Care - - - - 65

Physically Assessing the Patient - - - - 69

Assessing Laboratory and Patient Data - - - 75

III. ASSESSMENT OF KNOWLEDGE AND PRACTICES

Knowledge and Habits - - - - - - 81

Medication Administration - - - - - 91

Health Care Resources - - - - - - 95

IV. INTERVENTION

Individualizing Education Plans - - - - - 103

Instructional Methods - - - - - - - 113

Teaching and Counseling - - - - - - 117

Living with Diabetes - - - - - - - 125

Roles and Responsibilities - - - - - - 131

Metabolic Monitoring - - - - - - - 153

V. NUTRITIONAL PRINCIPLES AND GUIDELINES

The Diabetes Diet - - - - - - - - 155

The Acute Complications of Diabetes - - - - - 159

The Chronic Complications of Diabetes - - - - 171

The Pathophysiology of Diabetes - - - - - 172

Managing Care - - - - - - - - 172

Interpreting Research and Putting It into Practice - - - 180

VI. PROGRAM DEVELOPMENT AND ADMINISTRATION

The Diabetes Education Program - - - - - 183

VII. PRACTICE QUESTIONS - - - - 199

I. ASSESSMENT OF LEARNING

THE PHASES OF THE TEACHING AND LEARNING PROCESS

The phases of the teaching/learning process are the same as the phases of the nursing process: Assessment, diagnosis, planning, implementation, and evaluation.

- **Assessment**

  The purpose of assessment is to determine the patient's learning needs, their level of motivation and readiness, personal, ethnical and cultural aspects, age-specific characteristics and needs, barriers to learning (including cognitive impairments, language, level of comprehension or reading level and physical as well as psychological barriers to learning.) Simply stated, a learning need equals what the patient should know minus what the patient actually knows.

- **Diagnosis**

  The diagnosis phase includes the generation of a learning diagnosis based on analyzed assessment data. These diagnoses can include things like "A lack of knowledge about…", and "A knowledge deficit related to…".

- **Planning and Establishing Learning Goals or Objectives**

  The purpose of planning is to ensure that the patient and family teaching is consistent with identified learning needs, and that it can be evaluated in terms of effectiveness (outcome evaluation).

  Planning consists of generating objective and specific learning goals, among other things. Learning objectives are specific, measurable, behavioral, learner-centered, consistent with assessed need and congruent with the domain of learning. Examples of well-worded learning objectives are the "Patient will be able to list basic food groups" (cognitive domain) and the "Patient will demonstrate the correct use of a blood glucose monitor" (psychomotor).

- **Implementation**

  The implementation phase consists of conducting the education activity in an environment that is conducive to learning, which includes a physically comfortable environment as well as one that is trusting, open, respectful and accepting. Appropriate educational (including reading) materials are used based on the learning needs and characteristics of the learner, such as sensory impairments or learning styles.

- **Evaluation**

There are two types of evaluation in the teaching/learning process. They are referred to as formative and summative evaluation.

Formative evaluation is the continuous assessment of the effectiveness of the teaching while the teaching is being conducted. This allows the teacher to modify the plan as necessary.

Summative evaluation at the end of the learning activity allows the educator to determine whether or not the education has achieved the established learning objectives for the individual or group.

The Domains of Learning

There are three domains of learning that are the basis of all education, including patient and family education. These domains are:

- **The Cognitive Domain**

  This domain consists of both knowledge and understanding. An example of a cognitive domain patient outcome is, "The patient verbalized knowledge of all of their medications and side effects."

  The six levels of the cognitive domain from the basic to the most complex are knowledge, comprehension, application, analysis, synthesis and evaluation. Some of the teaching/learning strategies for this domain include online/computer based learning, peer group discussions, reading material and a discussion or lecture.

- **The Psychomotor Domain**

  The psychomotor domain consists of "hands-on skills" like taking blood pressure and using a blood glucose monitor correctly.

  The seven levels of this domain are perception, set, guided response, mechanism, complex overt response, adaptation and origination. Some of the teaching/learning strategies for this domain include demonstration, return demonstration and a video with a step-by-step demonstration of the psychomotor skill.

- **The Affective Domain**

  The affective domain includes the development of attitudes, beliefs, values and opinions. An example of affective domain competency is developing a belief that exercise is a valuable part of wellness.

There are five levels of the affective domain, which are receiving, responding, valuing, organizing and characterizing by a value or a value complex. The teaching/learning strategies for this domain include role-playing and values clarification exercises. The affective domain is rarely used for patient teaching.

Adult and Childhood Learning

Pedagogy is the term for childhood learning; andragogy is the term for adult learning. Unlike pedagogy, adult learning has immediate usefulness in terms of solving problems; it involves active learner involvement and participation. and the curriculum and content are based on the learner's needs and desires. Below is a table that compares and contrasts pedagogy and andragogy.

	PEDAGOGY	**ANDRAGOGY**
CURRICULUM	The state and the teacher develop and design the teaching, based on what they decide is important.	The learner, in collaboration with the diabetes educator, develops and designs the teaching, based on learner needs and other characteristics, such as their preferred learning style.
LEVEL OF INPUT	The child is a somewhat passive learner. The learner has a low level of involvement in all the phases of the teaching process.	The adult is a highly active learner. The learner has a high level of involvement in all the phases of the teaching process.
TEACHING METHODS	Homework & Teacher Lecture	Active learner participation The adult learner has a large amount of knowledge and experiences to share with others and to relate to the learning activity.
THE PURPOSE OF LEARNING	Childhood learning has little immediate application. This learning prepares the child for the future and their future needs.	Adult learning should have immediate application and usefulness. The learning aims to solve problems.

Overcoming Barriers to Learning

Some of the barriers to learning are discussed below.

- **Literacy**

    Sadly, many people in our nation are not able to read at all. Some may only be able to read and comprehend material at a low-grade level. Patient education material should be authored at or below a 6th grade reading level to accommodate for comprehension and literacy deficits.

    The diabetes educator must assess the patient's literacy level and provide learning materials that are appropriate to the patient in terms of their reading level so that the person is able to benefit from them.

- **Health Literacy**

    Patients are considered "health literate" when they are able to understand information and use it to make appropriate health care decisions. Almost 50% of patients are NOT health literate.

    Diabetes educators and other healthcare professionals must modify their communication and teaching to accommodate for low health literacy and to ensure comprehension. For example, simple anatomy and physiology information relating to diabetes is preferable to complex, biochemical explanations that the patient cannot understand. Additionally, the use of medical jargon and terminology should be avoided.

- **Motivation and Readiness**

    Patients will not learn unless they are motivated and ready to do so. Diabetes educators can motivate learners by involving them in the entire teaching/learning process, by focusing the learning on solving immediate and pressing concerns, and by explaining the benefits of learning in terms of problem resolution while maintaining an environment that is supportive of an open, honest and highly respectful learning environment.

    Motivation to learn and motivation to change are assessed as part of the assessment phase of the teaching process. Motivation will be further discussed later in this guide.

- **Learning Styles and Preferences**

    Whenever possible, individual learning styles and preferences should be accommodated for. Some learn best by listening, some by watching, some by reading and some by doing. Some like to read, or watch a video, or use a computer; others do not. Learning styles and preferences will be discussed later in this guide.

- **Cultural Aspects**

  Communication patterns, vocabulary, slang and/or terminology are differences that can separate members of a group, or culture, from those who are not members. Diabetes educators must become culturally competent about cultures, norms and gestures of others and also modify their terminology and behavior according to what is acceptable and understandable to the learner of a different culture.

- **Age-Specific Characteristics**

  Some examples of teaching modifications based on age are simple concrete and brief explanations for the toddler, simple and brief explanations for the pre-school child, the encouragement of questions and more detailed explanations for the school-age child, and adult-like teaching for the adolescent.

- **Language Barriers**

  Communicating with and teaching those who speak a language unlike our own is challenging. However, these barriers can be overcome to a great extent with some relatively simple techniques, such as speaking slowly, clarifying, reclarifying, using pictures and diagrams, and eliciting the help of an interpreter.

- **Health Beliefs**

  Health beliefs can also be a barrier to learning and changes in behavior. Patients who place a high value on health, health promotion and wellness will be more highly motivated to learn than those patients who do not place priority value on health, health promotion and wellness.

  Diabetes educators can overcome this barrier to learning by facilitating the patient's understanding of the importance of these values in terms of their diabetes and ways that the person can enhance their health, health promotion and wellness, despite the presence of the diabetes. These concepts will be further discussed later in this guide.

- **Religious and Spiritual Beliefs**

  Religious and spiritual beliefs can include the use of symbols, dreams, spiritual practices and beliefs, including those that are metaphysical in nature.

  For example, maintaining health may involve the use of proper clothing and proper diet (physical facet), the support of others including family members (psychological facet) and things like meditation, prayer and formalized religious practices (spiritual facet).

Similarly, health protection can be facilitated with symbolic clothing and special spiritual foods (physical facet), the avoidance of people and things that can lead to disease (psychological facet), and the use of religious customs, superstition, and amulets like the "Evil Eye" to ward off evil and harm (spiritual facet).

Lastly, the restoration of health is enabled with alternative healing methods, such as massage, herbs, homeopathic remedies and special foods (physical facet), exorcism, the use of culturally traditional healers, like medicine men and curanderos (spiritual facet), relaxation techniques (psychological facet) and religious rituals, such as special prayers.

- **Family Dynamics and Other Social Forces**

  Many diabetic patients have social support systems and family support; however, many do not. For example, the newly diagnosed diabetic patient may be widowed, single, geographically separated from family and friends and/or may not have family or friends that support them and their need for education and behavioral changes.

  The diabetic educator can increase social support systems by utilizing available community resources such as diabetic support groups, Meals on Wheels and transportation to and from healthcare related services, as indicated.

- **Psychological Factors**

  Diabetes educators and other healthcare professionals have to assess and accommodate for any actual or potential cognitive, sensory and psychological/emotional barriers to learning. For example, cognitive limitations can be overcome with slow, brief, simple and understandable explanations.

  Psychological barriers can be minimized by establishing trust, reinforcing learning with positive feedback, and minimizing stress. Moderate stress is a motivator; extreme stress and pain prevent learning. For this reason, extreme stress and pain should be addressed before the educational activity.

- **Physical Capabilities and Limitations**

  Sensory barriers can be accommodated by large print materials and Braille for the visually impaired, louder discussions with patients affected with a hearing loss, and the use of assistive devices like magnifiers, eyeglasses and hearing aids.

  Functional limitations can also impede learning. For example, a diabetic patient who has lost fine motor coordination may not be able to draw up their own insulin without the help of some assistive devices. Some of these assistive devices and their uses are discussed later in this guide.

Setting Learning Priorities Using Maslow's Hierarchy of Needs

Maslow's Hierarchy is used to establish priorities. Priority setting is useful to the diabetic educator. It allows the educator to address the highest priority teaching needs of the patient and significant others.

The following needs, according to Abraham Maslow, are listed from the highest to the lowest priority.

- **Physiological or Biological Needs**

  Physiological needs include hunger, thirst, sleep/rest, etc. Of all of these physiological needs, the needs for the ABCs (airway, breathing and cardiovascular function) are the greatest and highest priority.

- **Safety and Psychological Needs**

  The need for safety and security reflects the person's need for comfort, safety and security, which are some of the psychological needs that are included in this level.

- **Love and Belonging**

  This level reflects the person's need for love and belonging. Humans want to be accepted by others and to become, and remain, part of a group.

- **Self Esteem and Esteem by Others**

  Esteem needs reflect the person's need to achieve, to be competent, to gain the approval and recognition from others (esteem), also have their own feelings of self worth and self esteem.

- **Self Actualization**

  Self-actualization reflects the patient's need to reach their highest level of ability and potential. Not all individuals throughout their lifetimes achieve self-actualization.

Readiness to Change Behavior

- **Motivation**

  Patients will not learn unless they are motivated and ready to do so. Diabetes educators can motivate learners by involving them in the entire teaching/learning process, by focusing the learning on solving immediate and pressing concerns, by explain the benefits of learning in terms of problem resolution, and with the maintenance of an environment supportive of open, honest and highly respectful learning.

Motivation to learn and motivation to change are assessed as part of the assessment phase of the teaching process.

MOTIVATION, READINESS TO LEARN AND BEHAVIOR CHANGE

There are a wide variety of theories and models that can be highly useful to the diabetes educator in terms of their patients' needs, their readiness to change behavior, their level of motivation, their confidence in their ability to change, and the value of change.

- **Adaptation Models**

Adaptation models and theories address health as a function of how successfully the patient is able to flexibly cope and adapt when they are confronted with a health related problem. Disease occurs with maladaptation and health is facilitated with successful coping skills and healthy adaptation.

Diabetes education allows the person to cope with and adapt to their chronic disorder. The patient will be motivated to learn when they believe that they can cope with and manage their diabetes.

- **The Health-Illness Continuum: Ryan and Travis**

This model describes health and illness as ever changing states along a continuum with high-level wellness at one end of the continuum and high-level of illness and death, at the opposite end. The center of the continuum is a "neutral zone" which represents neither health nor illness.

Patients move along the continuum from illness toward health when they are successfully treated. Conversely, they can also move from a high level of wellness through the "neutral zone" to all degrees of illness when they are affected with an acute or chronic disorder, disease or health threat.

Diabetic patients can move along the continuum from illness toward health when they are successfully controlling their diabetes as the result of patient education.

- **Holistic Models of Health and Wellness**

Holistic approaches to health and wellness facilitate the diabetes educator's full understanding of the patient's physical, psychological, social, and spiritual status and all the simultaneous interrelationships of these dimensions within an ever-changing environment.

Changes in the patient lead to simultaneous changes in the environment as well as among the various other dimensions of the patient. The patient and the environment are both open systems with dynamic interactions and interrelationships of the parts.

Diabetes and uncontrolled diabetes occur as the result of several factors and addressing these multiple forces can control it. For example, the diabetic patient will benefit from education relating to exercise, diet, and medications since all of these factors impact on the patient within their environment.

- **The Dimensions Model**

This model is particularly useful to guide a complete and thorough assessment and the identification of needs based on all of these dimensions.

The six dimensions of health are:

1. Biophysical: Genetic composition, physical risk factors, and diseases

2. Psychological: Coping and mental health

3. Behavioral: Lifestyle choices like exercise and good nutrition

4. The physical environment: Air pollution and contaminated water supplies

5. Socio-cultural: Societal norms and beliefs

6. Health systems: Accessibility, availability and affordability of health care services.

This model is particularly useful to diabetes educators in terms of identifying and assessing the total patient and all of the factors that impact on the patient and their needs.

- **The Agent – Host – Environment Model: Clark and Leavell**

Disease occurs as the result of the interrelationships among the agent, the host and the environment.

The *agent* is any environmental factor or stressor that, with or without, their presence, can lead to disease. Some of these environmental factors can include biological, physical, chemical, mechanical, and psychosocial forces or stressors. For example, the genetic makeup of a patient can lead to diabetes; and the existence of healthy life style choices, like exercise and nutrition, facilitate wellness and the control of the diabetes.

The *host* is the patient, or patient. The host may or may not be at risk for an illness or disease. Some hosts are more susceptible and vulnerable than others. For example, factors like age and diet can affect the host's vulnerability and susceptibility to diabetes, for example.

The *environment* consists of all factors that are external, or extrinsic, to the patient. Some elements of the environment can place a person at risk for a disease or illness; other environmental factors predispose the person to wellness. For example, a social stressor such as the loss of a loved one can increase blood glucose levels.

- **The High-Level Wellness Model: Halbert Dunn**

This model consists of two axes (the horizontal health axis and the vertical environment axis) and four quadrants, which are called high-level wellness in a very favorable environment, emergent high-level wellness in an unfavorable environment, protected poor health in a favorable environment, and poor health in an unfavorable environment.

An example of *high-level wellness in a very favorable environment* is when a patient maintains a healthy lifestyle, actively participates in primary, preventive care and has the financial ability to do so.

An example of *emergent high-level wellness* in an *unfavorable environment* is when a patient's lack of ability to maintain a healthy lifestyle as the result of job and family responsibilities prohibit a favorable environment.

Protected poor health in a favorable environment occurs when a patient is ill, but they have access to health care services that address these needs. Access to health care services, including diabetes education, is a favorable environment that can facilitate wellness.

Poor health in an unfavorable environment is the most challenging of all of Dunn's grids. Poor health in an unfavorable environment is present when an ill person is in an unhealthy environment. For example, uncontrolled diabetic patients with poor nutrition who live in a community without fresh fruits and vegetables are an example of poor health in an unfavorable environment.

- **The Seven Components of Wellness: Anspaugh, Hamrick and Rosato**

The seven components of wellness are the physical, social, emotional, intellectual, spiritual, occupational and environmental components of health.

The *physical dimension* consists of things like overall functioning, fitness, and physical health.

The *social dimension* includes things like the initiation and maintenance of relationships, including social and intimate relationships.

The *emotional or psychological dimension* includes health and illness variables like personal insight, emotional stability, and realistic views of one's strengths, weakness and limitations.

The *intellectual dimension* is reflected in lifelong learning, personal growth and effective coping skills.

The *spiritual dimension*, which is not necessarily religious, is manifested when the patient has purpose and meaning in life.

The *occupational dimension* includes the patient's ability to get and maintain a job and balance their work life with their personal and social lives.

Lastly, the *environmental dimension* includes environmental factors that protect and promote health, such as the provision of basic safety, clean water and clean air.

The diabetes educator must assess and address all of these seven dimensions because they all affect the individual's state of wellness, health and illness.

- **The HEALTH Traditions Model**

The HEALTH Traditions Model is highly useful for meeting the cultural, ethnic, and spiritual, or religious needs of patients. According to the HEALTH model, the physical, mental or emotional, and spiritual aspects of health can be fulfilled in terms of maintaining health, protecting health, and restoring health.

The nine facets, or aspects, of health and some examples of each are listed below.

Mental and Emotional Aspects

1. Mental or Emotional Health Maintenance: Social support networks and relaxation techniques.

2. Mental or Emotional Health Protection: The avoidance of negative people and influences.

3. Mental or Emotional Health Restoration: Cultural healers, medicine men and other practices like exorcism.

Physical and Biological Aspects

1. Physical Health Maintenance: Exercise, diet, and healthy lifestyle choices.

2. Physical Health Protection: Special ethnical or cultural foods and symbolic attire.

3. Physical Health Restoration: Acupuncture, massage and homeopathic treatments.

Spiritual Aspects

1. Spiritual Health Maintenance: Prayer, meditation and formal religious ceremonies.

2. Spiritual Health Protection: Wearing a cross to protect against evil spirits.

3. Spiritual Health Restoration: Religious and spiritual rituals and ceremonies.

- **Health – Belief Model: Rosenstock and Becker**

This model addresses the relationships between the patient's perceptions, behaviors and health. This model can predict whether a person will engage in things like screening tests and patient education, such as those based on their personal and/or cultural perceptions and beliefs. The factors that affect health beliefs include personal perceptions, modifying factors and the likelihood of action.

Some of the *personal perceptions* that influence health are perceived seriousness, perceived susceptibility and perceived threat. Patients who perceive a health threat as serious, and one that they are susceptible to, will most likely be motivated to act in order to avoid the serious threat.

Factors that modify the patient's perceptions include things like structural barriers (the lack of accessible and affordable healthcare and the lack of culturally competent care within the system), demographics (gender, age, culture, race and ethnicity), psychosocial forces (peer pressure, the lack of support for healthy habits), and cues to action. These cues can be external like the illness of another family member, and also internal or innate. Some of the internal cues to action are discomfort and fear.

Patient motivation and readiness to learn are enhanced when the patient perceives diabetes as serious; they will most likely be motivated to act in order to avoid this serious threat. Patient education gives the patient the knowledge, skills and abilities to act in the appropriate manner to control this threat.

- **Pender's Health Promotion Model**

According to this model, health is the actualization of inherent and acquired human potential through goal-directed behavior. Human potential is maximized with goal-directed behavior that is motivated by the patient's commitment to action.

The patient's level of motivation and commitment are influenced by many factors including emotions, affect, behavior specific cognitions, the patient's prior experiences, personal characteristics, such as cultural characteristics, feelings of self-efficacy and the support of others.

Whenever possible, the diabetes educator should maximize the above impacting factors to change behavior.

- **The Self-Care Deficit Theory: Dorothea Orem**

This theory is based on the premise that patients can and want to care for themselves as much as possible. This self-care allows patients to recover more holistically and rapidly than those who do not perform self-care. The three types of systems that Orem identifies are the supportive-educative (developmental), partly compensatory, and the wholly compensatory systems.

The supportive-educative (developmental) system aims to provide patients with the support, assistance and care that they need to continue their independent self-care. The supportive-educative system include patient education relating to diabetes and diabetes control,

The wholly compensatory system meets the self- care needs of those patients who can perform some, but not all, self- care functions. For example, a conscious diabetes patient who has had a stroke can usually perform some, but not all, of their self-care activities.

Lastly, the wholly compensatory system provides all care to the patient because the patient is not able to perform any self-care. Infants, very young children and patients in a coma are examples of patients who need wholly compensatory care.

Self-care requisites, according to Orem, fall into one of three categories. These categories are:

1. Universal self-care requisites: These needs are inherent to and universal for all people. The need for food, air and water, are examples of some universal self-care requisites.

2. Developmental self-care requisites: These self-care requisites are maturational and situational in nature. For example, maturation needs vary across the age groups and they vary when a traumatic event or another situation, such as the diagnosis of diabetes, arises.

3. Health deviation self-care requisites: These requisites or needs occur as the result of a disease, disorder, illness and disability, such as diabetes and the occurrence of diabetes complications.

- **The Interpersonal Relations Model: Hildegard Peplau**

A diabetes educator will enter into a personal and therapeutic relationship with a patient when a need arises. The educator assumes multiple roles in this relationship, including the roles of surrogate, counselor, leader, teacher, and resource facilitator in this relationship.

The four phases of Interpersonal Relations Model that the diabetes educator -patient therapeutic relationship moves through are as follows:

1. *Orientation*

   The diabetes educator assesses the patient's needs and explains these needs and problems to the patient. The patient then asks the diabetes educator for help and support.

2. *Identification*

   The diabetes educator understands the patient's perspective and their interpretation of their problems. The patient acts dependently, independently or interdependently with the diabetes educator (relatedness).

3. *Exploitation*

   The patient is now able to use services and get benefit and value from these educational services, as based on the patient's interests and needs.

4. *Resolution*

   The patient is able to progress to new and higher level goals as they discard older resolved needs and fulfilled goals.

- **The Goal Attainment Theory: Imogene King**

This theory focuses on the processes that the patient uses to meet and achieve their goal(s). The diabetes educator and the patient collaboratively establish goals, they communicate information to each other and then this dyad (diabetes educator and patient) takes the necessary actions to achieve those goals. It includes fifteen concepts including things like self, stress, roles, communication and power, for example.

The patient, according to King, is a social being who has three fundamental needs. These needs are as follows:

1. The need for care when the patient is unable to care for themselves

2. The need for health information
3. The need for care to prevent illness

The ultimate goal of the diabetes educator-patient relationship is to help the patient achieve their goals in terms of attaining and maintaining health. By using Imogene King's Theory of Goal Attainment, a diabetes educator can more effectively work and motivate their patients to achieve these goals.

- **The Adaptation Model of Nursing: Sister Callista Roy**

The patient is a biopsychosocial human with interrelated systems (biological, psychological and social). Even though there is no absolute level of balance, the patient strives to attain and maintain an optimal balance between and among these interrelated systems and the outside world (environment).

Roy's four modes of an adaptation, which are relatively easy to understand, are:

1. The Physiologic-Physical Mode
2. The Self-Concept-Group Identity Mode
3. The Role Function Mode
4. The Interdependence Mode

- **The Human Caring Theory: Jean Watson**

Caring consists of the following 10 interventions, which are referred to formally as "carative" factors:

1. Developing a helping-trust relationship
2. Promoting transpersonal teaching-learning
3. Assisting with the gratification of biophysical and psychosocial human needs
4. Forming a humanistic-altruistic value system
5. Instilling faith-hope
6. Cultivating a sensitivity to self and others
7. Promoting expressions of positive and negative feelings
8. Using problem-solving for decision-making
9. Providing and maintaining a supportive, protective, and/or corrective mental, physical, societal, and spiritual environment
10. Allowing for existential-phenomenological-spiritual forces

- **Lewin's Forced Field Theory of Change**

Lewin's Forced Field Theory of Change is perhaps the most popular of all change theories. Lewin's change theory consists of unfreezing, freezing and refreezing, the three phases of change. Lewin also describes barriers to change and facilitators to change.

In order for change to occur, the force of the facilitators to change must be greater in strength than the barriers to change. In other words, the pluses must outweigh the minuses for change to occur.

This theory, as well as other change theories, helps the diabetes educator to understand how they can influence behavior changes and positive choices for the patient, most often as the result of patient and family education. It also assists the diabetes educator to understand and facilitate change in the organization within which they work.

The Unfreezing Stage of Change

During the unfreezing stage of change, there is awareness that there is a problem, need, or an opportunity that has to be addressed with some action. For example, the diabetes educator may observe that the current outcomes of care do not currently meet expectations, established benchmarks and/or evidence-based practices. The diabetes educator is aware that there is a problem, and that there is a need, or opportunity, for improvement.

This unfreezing process is challenging because many people, and groups, resist change and prefer the status quo. Resistance, nonetheless, can be overcome with things like motivational techniques, individual/group involvement and participation, and good communication. Humans are most apt to accept change when they understand that real benefits can result from the change.

The Freezing Stage of Change

The planned change is implemented during the freezing stage. Those affected with the change may experience feelings such as fear, uncertainty and resistance. These barriers, too, can be overcome with effective strategies like communication, education, and ongoing reinforcement of the fact that benefits will be realized with positive change and the control of one's diabetes.

The Refreezing Stage of Change

During the refreezing stage, the affected person has fully accepted and implemented the change. It becomes somewhat routine for them. Some of the factors that can positively affect this stage, in order to promote long lasting and sustained change, include support, continued positive reinforcement and the stabilization of the change. The diabetes educator also plays a highly critical role in the refreezing stage of change.

- **Havelock's Six Phases of Planned Change**

The six phases of Havelock's Six Phases of Planned Change are developing relationships, diagnosing the existing problem, collecting available resources, choosing a solution, garnering acceptance and stabilizing the change.

- **Lippitt, Watson and Westley's Seven Phases of Change**

The seven phases of change in Lippitt, Watson and Westley's Seven Phases of Change are patient awareness of the need for change, the development of a change agent/patient relationship, which includes the diabetes educator-patient relationship, defining the problem, establishing the goals, implementing the plan for change, accepting the change, and a change in the relationship between the change agent/patient.

- **Roger's Innovation-Decision Process**

The diabetes educator, as change agent, provides the patient with knowledge and information about the benefits of change during the five stages of Roger's Innovation-Decision Process, which are knowledge, persuasion, decision, implementation and confirmation.

- **Chaos Theory**

This change theory addresses the constantly changing environment that affects the patient as an open system. Diabetes educators have to always expect the unexpected and never assume that predicted outcomes will occur automatically.

Factors that Affect Motivation and Readiness

Some of the factors that affect motivation and readiness to learn are:

- Level of pain
- Level of stress
- Developmental level
- Perceived learning needs
- Attitudes

- **Level of Pain**

Patients who are in severe pain cannot learn. They are not motivated to learn, because they have unmet physical needs and they are also not capable of active participation in learning activities. When at all possible, the level of pain should be decreased prior to a teaching activity.

- **Level of Stress**

Contrary to popular belief, stress is essential to the maintenance of basic life functions and it is also essential and necessary for the motivation to learn. We do not breathe unless our body becomes stressed with increased levels of carbon dioxide; and we would not learn unless we are affected with stress and anxiety.

Moderate levels of stress and anxiety motivate learners to learn. However, high-level anxiety and stress is not conductive to learning. High stress interferes with the learner's ability to focus and concentrate on the issue at hand.

- **Developmental Level**

Some of the variables that are assessed and addressed in the developmental dimension of the teaching/learning process include communication techniques, motivational techniques, and teaching strategies, in addition to the principles of pedagogy and androgogy, which were discussed above.

Some examples of teaching modifications, as based on age, are simple concrete and brief explanations for the toddler, simple and brief explanations for the pre-school child, the encouragement of questions and more detailed explanations for the school age child, and adult-like teaching for the adolescent.

Further information about growth and development are included below.

- **Perceived Learning Needs**

As described above, many theories and models support the fact that motivation can be positively and negatively impacted by the patient's perceptions in terms of their overall needs and the benefits that they perceive can be derived from educational activities.

- **Attitudes**

Some patients have an external locus of control and others have an internal locus of control. Some patients with an external locus of control view their problems, such as diabetes, as something that occurs, because of external forces and something that they have no control over. Other patients are motivated by an internal locus of control, demonstrated by the patient who believes that they can control their diabetes and they will act accordingly in terms of necessary behavioral changes.

The locus of control can be moved from an external locus of control to an internal locus of control when the educator is able to convince the diabetic patient that they can, like so many other diabetic patients, successfully control and cope with their diabetes. The patient can then develop a "can do" attitude.

Strategies to Enhance Motivation and Readiness

Motivation and learning readiness are critical to the teaching-learning process. People will not learn unless they are motivated and ready to do so. Patients and family members can be motivated to learn when the diabetes educator utilizes the following strategies:

- Learning should be an extremely active and participative process.

- An explanation of the benefits of the learning to the patient and family members is highly motivating because the learner believes that the teaching can help them to solve problems, such as diabetes and the prevention of complications. Patients are motivated to learn when they believe they can solve problems as the result of the learning activity.

- Relate the new knowledge to the patient's past knowledge and experiences, so the learner can comfortably fit this newly gained knowledge, skills and abilities into their life and life style.

- Involvement of the learners in the entire teaching-learning process encourages, and motivates, the learner to learn. The learner must have input into ALL the aspects of the learning plan, needs assessment, the teaching session and the evaluation of the outcome.

- Focus the teaching/learning on the immediate problems and the concerns of the learner and family members. The diabetes educator should explain how the learning can be applied immediately to their life situation and their healthcare problem relating to diabetes and the control of it.

- Maintain an open, honest, and highly respectful environment for learning.

- Encourage the learner to debate, share and exchange their knowledge, ideas and past experiences with the diabetes educator and others. Small group teaching activities provide learners with these opportunities.

Learning Styles and Preferences

People have unique learning styles and learning preferences that can facilitate or impede learning. For example, auditory learners prefer and do well with patient education discussions, but visual learners do not get the same benefits from discussions; they prefer visual information using pictures and diagrams.

Some of the learning styles and preferences include:

- Active and reflective learners
- Sensing and intuitive learners

- Verbal, auditory and tactile learners
- Sequential and global learners

All of these learning styles differ in terms of the learners' strengths and weaknesses and in terms of their preferred form of learning. Most people, however, have a combination of learning styles. For example, a reflective learner can also have the characteristics of a verbal and/or sequential learner.

Active and Reflective Learners

- Active Learner Preferences: Active learners prefer to learn with active engagement, doing, discussions, and group projects. Lectures without physical activity are more difficult for active learners when compared to reflective learners.

  Tips for Active Learners: Use group discussion and study groups.

- Reflective Learner Preferences: Reflective learners prefer to learn by thinking about the learning and content material first. They prefer solitary work rather than group work.

  Tips for Reflective Learners: Encourage the learner to reflect on readings, contemplate applications and summarize material rather than the memorization of facts.

Sensing and Intuitive Learners

- Sensing Learner Preferences: Sensing learners prefer memorizing facts, detail oriented learning, and practical, real world oriented learning, rather than abstraction; they use reliable methods of problem solving and they do not expect unanticipated results.

  Tips for Sensing Learners: Seek out procedures and concepts that can transform abstract concepts in concrete and practical solutions.

- Intuitive Learner Preferences: Intuitive learners consider relationships among various pieces of information. They prefer novel and innovative ideas rather than learning by routine. They are tolerant, and welcoming, of abstractions, including mathematics, and a more rapid pace than sensors.

  Tips for Intuitive Learners: Encourage the learner to employ careful thought before answering a question and solving a problem. Encourage the learner to connect theoretical and abstract thinking to facts.

Visual, Verbal and Tactile Learners

- Visual Learner Preferences: Visual learners prefer, and learn best, when they see things. These learners benefit from flow charts, demonstrations, diagrams, medical models, and videos. Discussions are not the strategy of choice for visual learners. They benefit greatly from pictorial handouts and other visual strategies.

- Verbal Learner Preferences: Verbal learners, on the other hand, benefit from the spoken and written word. Discussions and lectures are preferred over demonstration and the use of pictures.

  Whenever possible, the diabetes educator should employ strategies that meet the individual learning style preferences and, when group learning is being used, the diabetes educator should employ both strategies to accommodate the needs and preferences of visual and verbal learners.

- Tactile Learner Preferences: Tactile learners tend to remember things by doing, rather than listening or reading. This type of learner tends to learn best from hands-on experimentation. This type of learner tends to excel in areas such as dance, athletics or other mobility or movement based activities.

  Tactile learners learn through imitation and practice. There is a tendency to have difficulties with reading and comprehension.

Sequential and Global Learners

Sequential learners learn best when the material is presented with logical, orderly and linear steps; global learners, on the other hand, move the content and material all around in a seemingly illogical and disorder manner until the learner makes connections among the pieces of information and then understands it.

Sequential learners follow logical steps to find a solution and to master the material. They are also able to explain how they solved a problem. Global learners have difficulty explaining why and how the problem was solved but, nonetheless, global learners tend to have the ability to rapidly solve complex problems.

Whenever possible, the diabetes educator should employ strategies that meet the individual learning style preferences and, when, group learning is being used, the diabetes educator should employ both strategies to accommodate the needs and preferences of both the visual and verbal learners.

ASSESSING DEVELOPMENTAL STATUS

Age and developmental stages are assessed not only to determine if the patient is at the expected level of development but also to modify all aspects of care, and communication, according to the patient's specific needs. Erik Erickson's developmental tasks and Piaget's stages of cognitive development are most often used for the framework of this assessment and data analysis, although there are other theories and frameworks that can be useful.

Erik Erikson

Erik Erickson proposed eight major stages of development and expected tasks along the life span from infancy to old age. People who are able to resolve their age-related tasks are successfully able to progress to the next task; however, barriers to personal development and unresolved issues occur when a person is unable to achieve their age-related task.

Diabetic educators must consider the major developmental challenges facing their patients and modify their care accordingly. These stages, developmental tasks and signs of unsuccessful resolution are listed below.

- **Age Group: Infant**

  Task: Trust
  Effects of the Lack of Resolution of the Task: Mistrust and a failure to thrive

- **Age Group: Toddler**

  Task: Autonomy, self control & will power
  Effects of the Lack of Resolution of the Task: Shame, doubt and a low tolerance for frustration

- **Age Group: Preschool**

  Task: Initiative, confidence, purpose and direction
  Effects of the Lack of Resolution of the Task: Guilt and fear of punishment

- **Age Group: School Age Child**

  Task: Industry, self-confidence and competency
  Effects of the Lack of Resolution of the Task: Fears about meeting the expectations of others and feelings of inferiority

- **Age Group: Adolescent**

  Task: Identity formation, sense of self

Effects of the Lack of Resolution of the Task: Role confusion and poor self-concept and self-esteem

- **Age Group: Young Adult**

  Task: Intimacy, affection and love
  Effects of the Lack of Resolution of the Task: Isolation and the avoidance of relationships

- **Age Group: Middle Aged Adult**

  Task: Generativity, productivity, and concern about others
  Effects of the Lack of Resolution of the Task: Stagnation, self-absorption and a lack of concern about others

- **Age Group: Older Adults**

  Task: Ego integrity, wisdom and views life with satisfaction
  Effects of the Lack of Resolution of the Task: Despair and feelings that life is meaningless

Jean Piaget

Jean Piaget's levels of cognitive development from birth until 12 years of age are used as a guideline for assessing infants and children in terms of their growth and development.

These levels and characteristics are described below:

- **Up to 2 Years of Age: Sensorimotor thought**

  This consists of six substages and it includes the development of the skills and abilities to manipulate concrete objects.

- **From 2 to 7 Years of Age: Preoperational and symbolic functioning**

  The development of language

- **From 7 to 11 Years of Age: Concrete operations**

  Logical reasoning and the ability to solve concrete problems

- **12 Years of Age and Older: Formal operations**

  Cognitive functioning is completely developed. The person is capable of abstract, logical and complex thought.

Sigmund Freud

Sigmund Freud developed the concepts of id, ego and superego as well as psychological defense mechanisms and five stages of growth and development. The id is an unconscious mechanism that operates in terms of instant gratification and instant pleasure; the ego is the person's sense of self that moderates and controls the id so the person can act in a legally and socially acceptable manner. The superego is the person's conscience. The superego develops as the result of age, cultural, parental and social factors.

The five stages of Sigmund Freud's stages of development are:

- The oral stage
- The anal stage
- The phallic stage
- The latency stage
- The genital stage

Robert Havighurst

This theorist developed six age groups and the physical, psychological and social tasks associated with each. Robert Havighurst's age periods and related developmental tasks are as follows:

- **Infancy and Early Childhood**

  This age group is learning how to eat, walk and control elimination. The infant or young child establishes psychological stability, relationships with family, siblings and others and is also able to separate right from wrong with the development of the conscience.

- **Middle Childhood**

  The child further develops in terms of conscience, morality and values systems. Physical skills are further developed and reading, writing and basic math are learned.

- **Adolescence**

  During adolescence, the teenager assumes feminine or masculine roles and they also develop more mature relationships with peers of both genders. During this age, the patient will also think about their future occupational and educational goals, and develop ethical guidelines for behavior.

- **Early Adulthood**

  Early adulthood is characterized with the selection of a mate, starting a family, managing the home and developing social and civic relationships.

- **Middle Age**

  The middle years are characterized with economic stability and adjusting to the changes of middle years, which include menopause and the "empty nest".

- **Later Maturity**

  During later years, older adults cope with retirement, a lower income level, losses of loved ones and changing physical health status.

Stella Chess and Alexander Thomas

Stella Chess and Alexander Thomas generated nine children's temperamental qualities that are demonstrated within the environment. These nine temperamental qualities include:

- **Activity level:** Does the child have a high level of restlessness or is the child more calm and quiet?

- **Sensitivity:** Is the child sensitive and reactive to external stimuli or are they somewhat unaware and oblivious to external stimuli?

- **Adaptability:** Does the child cope with and adapt to unanticipated changes or are they resistant to changes?

- **Intensity:** Does the child react in an intense and strong reaction to external stimuli or do they react in a less intense and minimal manner?

- **Distractibility:** Is the child able to focus and remain on task or is the child easily distracted with minor stimuli?

- **Approach/Avoidance and Withdrawal:** Does the child jump into things readily or are they somewhat more cautious and hesitant to act?

- **Persistence:** Does the child stick with an activity or task or do they tend to give up on it?

- **Regularity:** Does the child engage in patterns of behavior or is the child disorganized and random in terms of their behavior?

- **Mood:** Is the child somber and serious or is the child happy and cheerful?

Roger Gould

Roger Gould addresses seven stages of young to older adulthood. These stages include:

- **Stage 1: Ages 16 to 18**

  During this stage, the adolescent wants to separate from their parents.

- **Stage 2: Ages 19 to 22**

  Although the young adult has developed autonomy, they often fear returning to the family unit.

- **Stage 3: Ages 23 to 28**

  This young adult now feels comfortable, well defined and secure. They feel that they have to prove themselves to their family.

- **Stage 4: Ages 29 to 34**

  These young adults have established their career, marriage and even children. They no longer feel that they have to prove themselves to others.

- **Stage 5: Ages 35 to 43**

  This age group tends to self-reflect and examine values and life itself. This age group typically cares for their adolescent children and they begin to view their own life as finite.

- **Stage 6: Ages 44 to 50**

  An individual's personality is well established. They know about the finality of life.

- **Stage 7: Ages 51 to 60**

  These adults become somewhat concerned about their physical health. They also become less negative.

Lev Vygotsky

Lev Vygotsky describes cognitive development within the context of culture, social and historical forces. This theory is used to treat children with autism, learning disorders, and mental disabilities. This theory supports the benefits of teaching and learning with group discussions and group work.

Robert Peck

Robert Peck's theory focuses on the positive changes associated with the aging process. The three development tasks of Peck expand upon Erikson's old age phase of integrity versus despair.

These three developmental tasks include:

- **Ego Transcendence versus Ego Preoccupation**

  This task is associated with one's acceptance of one's own demise without fear rather than being consumed with hanging onto life.

- **Body Transcendence versus Body Preoccupation**

  The elderly person accepts their own physical, bodily declines and functioning rather than losing their sense of well-being, happiness and satisfaction.

- **Ego Differentiation versus Work Role Preoccupation**

  During these years, the patient readjusts to their retirement and they often begin to engage in ego rewarding activities like golf and other social events and interactions.

II. ASSESSMENT OF STATUS

COLLECTING HEALTH HISTORY DATA

The purpose of the health history is to elicit data and information relating to the patient's current and past states of health, illness and wellness.

This data can be primary or secondary data. Primary data is provided by the patient while secondary data is collected from other sources, such as previous medical records and laboratory test results.

Data can also be classified as subjective and objective. Subjective data is not measurable or observable and it typically consists of the patient's own words. For example, a statement from the patient about their pain is an example of subjective data. Objective data, on the other hand, is empirically observable and measurable. Vital signs and blood glucose levels, for example, are objective data.

Lastly, data can be quantitative or qualitative. Quantitative data consists of numbers; qualitative data, unlike quantitative data, consists of words. The amount of sodium or potassium in the patient's blood is quantitative data; and the patient's beliefs and perceptions are examples of qualitative data.

The health history consists of several components:

- Demographics or biographical data
- Chief complaint
- Past medical history
- Current medical history
- Family medical history
- Cultural history
- Spiritual history
- Lifestyle choices
- Social data
- Psychological status
- Patterns of health care

During the interview process, the diabetes educator must establish trust, inform the patient and their significant others about the purpose of the health history, insure patient confidentiality, and maintain patient privacy, and a comfortable environment.

During the interview, open-ended questions and closed ended questions are used. Open-ended questions elicit full and meaningful answers from the patient that reflect the patient's own beliefs, knowledge and feelings; closed ended questions do not elicit the same rich information and data. Closed ended questions simply elicit a "no" or "yes" response and no other information. An example of an open-ended question is "Tell me about your pain"; and an example of a closed ended question is "Are you in pain?" Open-ended questions are preferred during the collection of health history data.

- **Demographic and Biographical Data**

  Examples of this data include the patient's name, address, phone number, occupation and cultural values and beliefs.

- **Chief Complaint**

  The chief complaint is elicited from the patient by asking a question such as, "What brings you to the emergency room today?" or "What brings you to the hospital today?" These questions are open-ended.

  The responses to these questions will reflect the patient's perception of their current situation. Please note: The patient's response may or may not be accurate, but nonetheless, these perceptions are helpful to diabetes education even when they are inaccurate. They still provide indicators relating to the patient's level of understanding and their level of insight, both of which provide baseline data to determine the patient's educational needs.

- **Past Medical History**

  This component of health history collects data relating to:

  - Immunization status
  - Childhood illnesses
  - Acute illnesses
  - Chronic illnesses
  - Past injuries and accidents
  - Current medications, including over-the-counter medications, herbs and supplements
  - Prior surgical procedures
  - Previous hospitalizations
  - Allergies (medications, foods, environmental sources)
  - Previous healthcare adverse events like medication toxicities and the adverse effects of anesthesia

- **Current Medical History**

  Some of the questions asked during this phase of the health history include:

  - What are your symptoms?
  - When did the symptoms begin?

- What precipitates it?
- What relieves it?
- What makes it worse?
- How often does this problem or the symptoms occur?
- How long does it last?
- Where is the pain or distress?
- Tell me the character (crushing, sore, etc.), intensity (on a pain scale from 1 to 10), the quality (color of the sputum, etc.), the quantity (amount of drainage, etc.) of the presenting symptom or concern.
- Do you have any complications relating to diabetes?

- **Family Medical History**

  During this phase of the health history, the diabetes educator collects data and information about the family's presence or absence of common disorders, such as:

  - Genetic disorders (bleeding, clotting, etc.)
  - Alcoholism
  - Hypertension
  - Cancer
  - Diabetes
  - Heart disease
  - Other psychological and social disorders and concerns, both acute and chronic, as well as the ages and current states of health, or age and cause of death for grandparents, parents, siblings and children.

- **Cultural History**

  Some of the cultural data collected during this phase of the health history include the person's ethnic and cultural customs, beliefs, practices and preferences. Similar to age/development status, personal preferences, personal beliefs, and religious/spiritual needs, care must be modified according to the patient's cultural history.

- **Spiritual History**

  Some of the data and information collected during this phase of the health history include the person's religious and spiritual customs, beliefs, practices and preferences. Spirituality and religion are different concepts.

- **Lifestyle Choices**

  The diabetes educator collects this data and information in order to identify possible risk factors and to provide a foundation for future teaching and health promotion activities.

- Diet, dietary practices, dietary patterns and level of nutrition including any dietary restrictions, the quality and quantity of food consumed, cultural preferences, and religious modifications

- Strengths and weaknesses in terms of the patient's performance of the activities of daily living, such as dressing, eating, grooming, bathing and hygiene

- Consumption patterns in relationship to illicit drugs, alcohol, and tobacco

- Sleep and rest patterns

- Exercise

- Occupational and vocational preferences

- **Sociocultural Data**

  Examples of sociocultural data are economic status, level of education, employment, family composition, support systems, such as family members, friends and community based resources, income levels, types of employment, including hazardous jobs, home and neighborhood situations and conditions, including environmental and safety risks, social norms, and the accessibility of health care and public transportation.

- **Psychological Status**

  Some of the psychological data collected during the health history include things like the patient's:

  - Attitude, mood, affect, thought processes and coherence
  - Coping skills and mechanisms and their successes or failures
  - Stress and stressors
  - Communication patterns
  - Any history of a chronic or acute psychological disorder, such as depression, abuse, neglect, violence, apathy, suicidal thoughts, and panic disorders

- Patterns of Health Care

  The purpose of eliciting data and information about the patient's patterns of health care is to determine what type of healthcare resources they utilize. For example, does the patient use a primary care physician, a community clinic, specialists, etc.? Are these resources adequate and accessible for the patient?

ASSESSING MEDICATION REGIMENS

Diabetes educators assess their patients in terms of their medication regimen. This assessment includes the names, dosages and frequency of prescription and nonprescription drugs, all herbals and alternative remedies, and a history of any allergies, side effects, adverse reactions, toxicities, etc.

Basic Medication Terms and Definitions

- *Chemical name:* The chemical composition of the drug.

- *Trade or brand name:* The manufacturer's name for the drug. Trade name drugs are more expensive than generic drugs.

- *Generic name:* The name of a drug that can include a number of different trade names. For example, metoprolol, which is a generic name can have equivalent trade names such as Lopressor and Metoprolol Succinate ER.

- *Drug absorption:* Absorption occurs as the medication moves through the digestive tract. Rates of absorption vary according to the acidity of the stomach's fluids and the presence of food, for example.

- *Drug distribution:* After absorption, the components of the medication move in the bloodstream to the intended target.

- *Drug metabolism or biotransformation:* The breakdown of a drug, or medication, in the liver.

- *Excretion:* Most drugs are excreted through the kidney, but some are also excreted with feces and respiratory expiration.

- *Therapeutic or desired effect:* A therapeutic effect is the primary, expected effect of a specific medication. For example, the therapeutic effect of metoprolol is to lower blood pressure.

- *Side effects:* A side effect of a medication is a secondary, not primary, effect of a medication. Some side effects are desirable, others are minor, and some can be extremely serious.

- *Idiosyncratic effects:* An idiosyncratic effect of a medication is an unexpected side effect that is peculiar and specific to a particular patient. When a sedative makes a person agitated, rather than sedated, this is an idiosyncratic effect.

- *Cumulative effects:* The buildup of the medication in the patient's system as a result of impaired excretion or metabolism of the drug, which can lead to toxic effects.

- *Adverse effects:* The most serious side effects of drugs that lead to immediate discontinuation of the medication; adverse effects must be reported.

- *Drug toxicity:* An overdose of a medication that occurs when the patient's metabolism and/or excretion is impaired.

- *Interactions:* Medications can interact with a number of things. Some interactions include those with other medications including "over the counter" drugs, foods, lifestyle choices, like alcohol use, herbs and other natural remedies.

- *Potentiating effect:* A synergistic effect results from the combination of two or more drugs, herbs, and/or alternative remedies where the effects of one or more are increased.

- *Inhibiting effect:* An inhibiting effect is one that results from the combination of two or more drugs, herbs, and/or alternative remedies where the effects of one, or more are decreased.

- *Drug allergy:* An antigen- antibody immunologic response to a medication. All patients must be assessed for any drug sensitivities or allergies. Any allergies or sensitivity to medications must be documented.

- *Anaphylactic reaction:* This is the most severe of all medication allergy responses, and it can be life-threatening. The throat and tongue swell, obstructing the airway.

- *Drug tolerance:* This often occurs when a patient has been receiving an opioid for an extended period of time. The patient needs increasing doses of the drug in order to achieve the therapeutic effect.

- *Drug interaction:* Drugs can interact with a number of things including other prescribed drugs, over the counter drug, foods, herbs, and other natural substances.

The Uses, Contraindications, Precautions and Side Effects Associated with Medications

All medications have intended uses, or indications for use. When a medication is used for a purpose not specified and approved, this use is referred to as "off-label use".

Some medications are contraindicated for certain patients. For example, a medication can be contraindicated, or prohibited, for patients who are pregnant, lactating, and/or have severe renal disorders, such as occurs among diabetic patients with renal failure, or hepatic disease.

The most commonly occurring contraindication is an allergy or sensitivity to a medication. The patient's allergies must be assessed and known by the diabetic educator.

Other medications have known precautions. For example, a medication may be used with caution among the diabetic population. When a decision to use this medication is made, despite the precaution, it is particularly important to monitor and assess the patient's responses to the medication.

All medications have side effects, but some are more serious than others. Nausea and vomiting are the most commonly encountered side effects. Some side effects are just annoying, while others can be life-threatening. Some medications also have toxic effects. For example, tinnitus is a sign of toxicity associated with aspirin.

Assessing Treatment Fears and Concerns

During the assessment phase, the diabetic educator assesses treatment fears and concerns. Many diabetic patients are fearful and concerned about hypoglycemia, hyperglycemia, needles, weight gain, changes in life style and other things.

All of the patient's fears and concerns can be resolved and decreased with effective patient education. The table on the next page shows some content that can, and should be, presented to the patient for each of these fears and concerns.

COMMONLY OCCURRING FEARS AND CONCERNS	TEACHING CONTENT TO ALLEVIATE THE FEAR AND RESOLVE THE CONCERNS
Hypoglycemia	- The causes of hypoglycemia - Balancing exercise, diet and medication - Strategies to prevent hypoglycemia - The signs and symptoms of hypoglycemia - Actions to reverse the hypoglycemia - Commonly occurring events and situations that can lead to hypoglycemia (diet, exercise and medications)
Hyperglycemia	- The causes of hyperglycemia - Balancing exercise, diet and medication - Strategies to prevent hyperglycemia - The signs and symptoms of hyperglycemia - Commonly occurring events and situations that can lead to hyperglycemia (diet, exercise and medications)
Needle Phobia	- Anatomy and physiology of the skin and subcutaneous tissue - Injection site and the rotation of injection sites - Practice drawing up sterile water and injecting it into a medical model or an orange - Drawing up and self-injecting insulin
Weight Gain	- The importance of a regular, healthy diet - The role of exercise in weight gain and weight loss
Life Style Changes	- Assess the patient's current life style (eating out, vacations, etc.) - Teach the patient how to maintain their current life style patterns and choices and recommend some modifications to it.

ASSESSING SUPPORT SYSTEMS AND CONSUMPTION HABITS

Support Systems

The diabetic educator must thoroughly, completely and accurately assess each member of the family, the dynamics within the family unit and other social support systems that can be helpful to the diabetic patient.

All families are unique and different, and all members of the family unit are also unique and different in terms of their physical, social, emotional, intellectual, spiritual, and occupational dimensions, strengths and weaknesses.

Some families have all members of the family who are physically, socially, emotionally, intellectually and occupationally able and willing to support the diabetic patient and assist in their care. Most families, however, are not this fortunate.

Members of the family may simply not want to help and support the patient; others may not be physically or emotionally capable of caring for their diabetic loved one. For example, an elderly woman with multiple health problems and profound emotional and cognitive problems, like dementia, cannot care for her diabetic husband.

Still other family members may be geographically distant from their loved one with diabetes so they, even when they are physically, emotionally, and cognitively able to support the patient, cannot support the needs of the patient because geographic distance prohibits this involvement. Similarly, the "sandwich generation" that has children and parents to care for may be employed and not able to leave their job and continue to support themselves while caring for a diabetic family member.

In these cases, the diabetic educator, often in collaboration with a social worker, will identify resources within the community that can assist the patient. Some of these community support systems may include civic and religious groups, governmental agencies and services like Meals on Wheels and medically necessary transportation.

Consumption Patterns

- **Nutrition**

    A patient's nutritional status can be influenced by their age or level of development, gender, ethnicity and cultural beliefs in regards to food, personal preferences, religious practices, health problems, lifestyle, economics, and psychological factors. The consumption assessment includes all of these factors.

    The age and development status of the patient affects their nutritional needs. For example, adolescents require more calories than elderly people, because of their rapid growth and development. Gender sometimes also affects nutritional preferences.

Different ethnicities, cultures, and individuals within a culture can have different preferences regarding food. There may also be variances in terms of the amount of food consumed as well.

Furthermore, food and dietary preferences are influenced by a patient's belief about foods, such as eating a specific cereal because of a commercial or advertisement that offers better health. Some patients choose to follow a fad diet that promises quick weight loss. These choices and decisions are all assessed.

There are often religious beliefs that influence a patient's diet as well. For example, Muslims do not eat pork and other religions forbid consuming alcohol, coffee, tea or meat.

Nutrition is also influenced by lifestyles. For example, those who work outside of the home may choose to eat fast foods, which are mostly unhealthy, because they do have the time or desire to cook when they come home from work. Others may opt for healthier foods that can be prepared in their homes.

Economic issues also affect a patient's nutrition status. For example, some are unable to afford fresh fruits or vegetable. There are also patients who live without a stove and/or refrigerator, thus leaving the diabetic patient with no choices other than eating out, which most often means that the patient will eat less expensive fast foods rather than more expensive, but healthier, freshly prepared meals.

Health conditions, such as swallowing disorders, affect a patient's nutritional status. Other health disorders that can affect a patient's nutritional status include nausea, vomiting, diarrhea, diabetes, hypertension, and a number of others. The assessment process includes assessing all of these factors.

Psychological disorders that can affect a patient's nutritional status include anorexia and bulimia, which are most common in adolescent females. Depression, loneliness and stress also affect a patient's nutritional status.

- **Hydration**

It is necessary for all patients to be assessed for excesses and deficits in terms of hydration and nutrition. Fluid volume excesses are referred to as hypervolemia. There are several causes for hypervolemia including renal problems, liver disease, heart failure, excessive fluid intake and high dietary sodium, which retains fluid.

Weight gain, increased central venous pressure, hypertension, rales, shortness of breath, distended neck veins, bounding pulse, edema and tachycardia are all signs of hypervolemia.

Hypovolemia, a fluid deficit, can be caused by decreased fluid intake, vomiting, diarrhea, anorexia, impaired swallowing, fever, and polyuria, which is excessive urine production.

Weight loss, hypotension, low body temperature, a weak thready pulse, postural hypotension, poor skin turgor, dry mucus membranes, sunken eyeballs, flat neck veins, scant urinary output, and increased blood urea nitrogen (BUN), hematocrit and urinary specific gravity are all signs of hypovolemia

ASSESSING PSYCHOSOCIAL AND MENTAL HEALTH

The term mental health can have many definitions. For example, mental health can be defined as successful adjustments to and coping mechanisms for the stressors of everyday life in a manner that is acceptable to society and healthy for the patient. Mental illness, on the other hand, is defined as the lack of effective adjustments and coping skills to deal with the stressors of everyday life in an acceptable manner and healthy manner.

Some of the factors that affect the development of mental health include genetic makeup (inheritance), life circumstances, such as good physical health and friends, and nurturing during the early years of life.

Patients who have diabetes and those with a new diagnosis of diabetes are often impacted with psychosocial and mental health forces.

Risk Factors Associated With Mental Illness

- **Populations at Risk**

  Adolescents are often adversely affected with sexual identity issues, peer pressure, illicit drug use and bullying.

  New parents often experience stressors relating to the transition from being a couple to being parents with great responsibilities, possible loss of financial income, anxiety regarding the child's well-being, concerns that they are not adequate parents, the baby's constant demands and needs, as well as some conflicts and ambivalence about accepting the pregnancy and the newborn.

  Older adults may be at risk because of social isolation, grief/loss after the death of a spouse, friend, or another loved one, fear of declining physical and mental abilities, actual physical and mental declines, reduced income, and relocation to another level of care like an assisted living or long-term healthcare facility.

- **Gender**

  Women are at greater risk than males for mental illness as a result of increased risk of domestic violence, hormonal changes, pregnancy, and internal or intrapersonal conflicts about the roles they wish to fulfill in terms of career, motherhood and more.

- **Other Illnesses and Disorders**

  The physically ill and the cognitively impaired are at risk for mental illness because they are affected with social isolation, lack of independence, a poor quality of life, impaired self image, societal stigma and the lack of meaningful relationships.

Patients with diabetes, for example, may be affected with mental disorders such as depression, anxiety and grief.

- **Social Forces**

    The homeless and refugees have stressors, such as financial uncertainty, poverty, poor social status, a loss of self-esteem and self-worth, as well as other stressors.

The Signs and Symptoms of Mental Illness

Commonly occurring signs and symptoms of mental illness are not as clear and objective as the signs and symptoms of a physiological disorder.

The signs and symptoms of mental disease can include social withdrawal, changes in personal habits like grooming and hygiene, abnormal changes in mood, changes in thought processes, and other behaviors.

The Classifications of Mental Illness

The American Psychiatric Association's (APA) *Diagnostic and Statistical Manual of Mental Disorders (DSM)* contains four major categories of mental illness. Each of these four broad categories contains hundreds of related mental health disorders and their characteristics.

The APA's four major categories are:

- **Mood disorders**

    These disorders affect the patient's mood. These disorders are also referred to as mood affective disorders.

- **Behavioral disorders**

    Patients with behavioral disorders typically exhibit hostility, aggression and defiance. These people can experience problems at home, at school, at work, and in other social settings as a result of their behaviors.

- **Thought disorders**

    These patients have disordered thoughts. They have serious problems with thinking, feeling and behavior.

- **Mixed disorders**

    These disorders have features of more than one of the above.

Some of the most commonly occurring psychological and emotional alterations associated with diabetes and other chronic diseases include anxiety, depression, grief and loss, alterations of bodily image, loss of control, coping and coping skills.

- **Anxiety**

  Anxiety affects the patient with feelings of dread, discomfort, and apprehension. Anxiety leads to autonomic responses and the anticipation of danger.

  The signs and symptoms of anxiety include:

  o Affective signs and symptoms: Increased helplessness, irritability, fright and worry

  o Behavioral signs and symptoms: Insomnia and vigilance

  o Sympathetic signs and symptoms: Anorexia, increased blood pressure and pulse

  o Physiological signs and symptoms: Diaphoresis and trembling

  o Parasympathetic signs and symptoms: Fatigue, urinary changes, weakness and faintness

  o Cognitive changes: Poor problem solving skills and a lack of an adequate attention span

- **Depression**

  Depression, of varying degrees, often affects the patient and those close to the patient when they are affected with a serious illness like diabetes. Depression leads to physical, emotional and cognitive changes.

  The signs and symptoms of depression include:

  o Feelings of hopelessness and helplessness
  o Feelings of poor self-esteem and worthlessness
  o Sadness and despair
  o Dejection
  o Insomnia and sleep loss
  o Listlessness
  o Weight loss and anorexia
  o Social withdrawal
  o Lack of sexual desire
  o Poor levels of concentration, poor decision making and problem solving skills, and diminished performance

At times, a depressed patient is at risk for suicide. All threats of suicide must be taken seriously. The ultimate goal of treatment for these patients is to prevent suicide and return the patient to the community when they are safe to do so without any continued risk for self-harm.

The care for and treatment of a depressed patient is multifaceted. The patient needs social support, perhaps spiritual support, cognitive behavioral therapy, and sometimes needs medications such as antidepressants. They often also benefit from non-pharmacological approaches such as stress reduction and relaxation techniques.

- **Grief and Loss**

Loss, often associated with grief, is multidimensional. Loss can be actual, perceived, or anticipated. It occurs when a person has a significant change that causes the loss of something of value or when the person anticipates and/or perceives the loss of something of value.

Sources of loss can originate from many things, including a loss of self and one's bodily image because of the signs and symptoms of their diabetes as well as extrapersonal losses like the loss of a home in a fire, and the loss of savings with a hospitalization and diabetes care. All losses impact on the patient.

Perceived losses are those losses that are not verifiable by others. The patient with a perceived loss experiences feelings of grief because they perceive a loss despite the fact that is not actually occurring. For example, an elderly woman may perceive that she is no longer useful to others, when in fact the woman is still actively engaging in social and charitable activities. This perception, although faulty, still affects the person.

People have anticipatory grief and loss before an actual or perceived loss actually occurs. This is known as *saudade*, which is Portuguese for "the anticipation of longing." For example, a son may undergo severe anticipatory loss and grief soon after his mother has been diagnosed with diabetes. Similarly, a woman may have anticipatory loss and grief relating to her loss of a diabetes-related infected limb.

- **Theories and Conceptual Frameworks Relating to Grief and Loss**

  o **Kubler Ross's Stages of Grieving**

    Similar to the other theories of loss, grieving and death, Kubler Ross's stages of grieving include:

    - Denial
    - Anger

- Bargaining
- Depression
- Acceptance

Bargaining is a unique phase of this theory. During the bargaining stage, the patient negotiates and bargains to avoid the loss. Spiritual support is often helpful during this stage.

- **Engel's Stages of Grieving**

  According to Engel, the stages of grieving are:

  - Shock and disbelief
  - Developing awareness
  - Restitution
  - Resolving the loss
  - Idealization
  - Outcome

  During shock and disbelief, the patient denies the loss and refused to accept it. Later the patient consciously acknowledges the loss and may even express anger towards others including family members and healthcare professionals like the diabetes educator.

  During the resolution stage, the patient contemplates the loss and then the patient may accept a dependent role in terms of their support network. Patients deify and idealize the lost loved one and may also experience guilt and ambivalence.

  During the outcome phase of Engel's model, the patient adjusts to the loss as based on their characteristics and the characteristics of the loss, as discussed above.

- **Sander's Phases of Bereavement**

  The phases of bereavement, according to Sander's theory, are:

  - Shock
  - Awareness of the loss
  - Conservation and withdrawal
  - Healing- the turning point
  - Renewal

  These phases are quite similar to those of Engel with some variations. For example, during the conservation and withdrawal phase, the person will withdraw from others and attempt to restore their physical and emotional well-being; and during the healing stage, the person will move from emotional distress to the point where they are able to learn how to live without the loved one. During the renewal phase, the person is able to live independently of the loved one.

- **Alterations of Bodily Image**

Alterations of bodily image commonly occur with chronic and long-term illnesses. Some of these alterations are objective and others are subjective. For example, objective physical alterations can occur with a loss of a body part or an alteration of the appearance of a body part. The surgical amputation of a leg is an objective, physical alteration of body image. On the other hand, alterations of bodily image can occur as the result of the patient's subjective, intrapersonal, perceptions of self and body image.

Alterations of bodily image can lead to things like the avoidance of the body part and the nonverbal and verbal expression of actual and perceived alterations. As with all other aspects of care, diabetes educators should assess the patient's perceived and actual body image. Some tools, like the Body Image Quality of Life Inventory, quantitatively measure the patient's quality of life, as well as the negative and positive influences of body image on the diabetic patient's quality of life.

Some of the appropriate interventions for impaired and altered body image include acknowledging the patient's beliefs and perceptions and encouraging the patient to express their feelings openly in a trusting relationship.

- **Loss of Control**

Humans strive for control, autonomy, and independence in all aspects of their life. These factors often change when illness and disease occur. These losses, like other losses, can lead to grief and grieving.

The loss of control and independence can result from physical, psychological and social forces. For example, a patient with diabetes may lose a degree of independence, and they can also lose control over their destiny and their bodily changes. Similarly, a patient may experience psychological depression, which affects their life and their quality of life. Still more may lose control in the social arena. They may no longer be able to provide financial support for their family and they may lose control in terms of their interpersonal relationships and roles, including intimate relationships.

Diabetes educators must assess the patient's psychological feelings relating to the loss of their independence, autonomy, and control. All patients should be encouraged to be as independent as possible in terms of decision-making and self-care activities. All physical, psychological and social barriers should be identified and eliminated to the greatest extent possible.

- **Stress, Coping and Coping Skills**

Stressors can be biophysical, emotional or psychological, social, spiritual, cultural, and intellectual. Stressors can also be classified as intrinsic, innate or internal, in contrast to extrinsic and external stressors. Stressors have to be coped with or they can lead to many complications, including anxiety, physiological alterations and depression.

According to the adaptation models of health, health is a function of how successfully the patient is able to flexibly cope when they are faced with a health-related problem. Disease occurs with maladaptation; health is facilitated with successful coping skills. Coping methods can be healthy and adaptive; other coping strategies are unhealthy and maladaptive.

During the assessment phase, the patient and family coping patterns are assessed in terms of whether or not they are effective and healthy. Maladaptive coping patterns, like the abuse of alcohol and illicit drugs, have to be eliminated and more successful and healthy coping patterns have to be developed. For example, stress and relaxation techniques may be taught and encouraged, and the patient may need the diabetes educator's support to identify their strengths so they can be further developed.

ASSESSING BARRIERS TO SELF-CARE

Similar to some of the barriers associated with the teaching/learning process, diabetes educators have to assess and identify barriers to diabetes self-care. The diabetes educator must address, eliminate and or minimize these barriers after they are assessed and identified.

Some of these barriers include those associated with cognitive ability, language, cultural impacts, psychosocial status, physical abilities, and economic status.

- *Cognitive Barriers*

  Some patients with diabetes are not able to perform diabetes self-care because their cognitive abilities, and those of a caregiver, may be impaired.

  For example, a young child may not be fully able to comprehend self-care procedures because of their developmental status. A developmentally challenged teenager, an older person with Alzheimer's dementia, a deeply lethargic or comatose patient, and patients with a previous closed head injury that alters cognitive ability are all examples of patients who are limited in terms of their performance of diabetes self-care, because their cognitive abilities and level of cognition are impaired.

- *Level of Motivation*

  Some patients are simply just not motivated to perform diabetes self-care. A small number of patients enjoy the "sick role"; they want and/or expect others to provide care to them. These patients should be encouraged to, at least minimally, participate in diabetes self-care, because self-care is helpful to the patient in many ways, including the enhancement of the patient's self-esteem and their quality of life.

- *Cultural Aspects*

  Some cultures fully support self-care and others do not. For example, some cultures rely on females to provide care to others; other cultures believe that the elders should be cared for by the younger generation. Still more cultures do not value self-care and the members of the culture rely on others, such as medical professionals and medicine men, to provide care to their members who are ill or affected with a chronic disorder such as diabetes.

- *Language Barriers*

  Although language barriers do not directly affect the patient's ability to perform diabetes self-care, language barriers often influence the communication and teaching processes that are necessary for successful diabetes management.

Nonetheless, language barriers can be overcome by speaking slowly, clarifying, reclarifying, using pictures and diagrams, and eliciting the help of an interpreter.

- *Psychosocial Barriers*

Diabetes patients who are affected with psychological and social barriers to diabetes self-care are challenging for the diabetes educator. However, these barriers can also be overcome. For example, patients affected with a psychological condition like depression or other mental health disorders, as described above, may need psychological help and support so they can begin to participate actively in their own self-care. Similarly, a patient without family and other social support systems may need referrals to community resources that can minimize the adverse effects of this isolation from others.

- *Physical Barriers*

Physical impairments and disabilities often affect the level of diabetes self-care that the patient is able to perform. For example, visually impaired patients may not be able to see how much insulin to draw up; those with a hearing impairment may not benefit from verbal education relating to diabetes self-care; and patients who have had a stroke that impairs their ability to use one arm and hand will not be able to manipulate insulin and inject themselves. Some assistive devices to overcome these barriers are discussed in full later in the text.

- *Economic Barriers*

The lack of personal resources and a lack of health insurance can negatively affect a person's ability to not only provide diabetes self-care, but also to purchase necessary medical care, medications, equipment and supplies like needles and blood glucose monitoring test strips.

Social services may be able to help patients who have economic barriers to diabetes care and diabetes self-care.

PHYSICALLY ASSESSING THE PATIENT

In addition to the health history assessment discussed earlier, diabetes educators must also be able to physically assess diabetes-specific functions, signs and symptoms.

This includes assessing:

- The lower extremities
- Insulin injection sites
- Blood glucose monitoring sites
- Blood pressure
- Height and weight
- Body mass index
- Skin alterations

Some skin alterations include sores, ulcers and other unusual conditions like *acanthosis nigricans*, which is a skin condition that appears as dark areas of the skin, and velvety discoloration in a patient's skin creases and/or body folds. It most commonly occurs in a patient's armpits, groin and/or neck. This skin disorder is most common among patients who are obese and/or have diabetes.

Physical Assessment Methods and Techniques

The four basic methods or techniques used for physical assessment are:

- *Inspection:*

  Inspection is the purposeful and systematic visual inspection and examination of the patient. Inspection is typically the first aspect of assessment when performing a total, head to toe assessment of the patient's body.

- *Palpation:*

  The palpation technique employs the sense of touch. There are two varieties: Light palpation and deep palpation. Light palpation is used more often than deep palpation because deep palpation is potentially dangerous to the patient and must be used with caution.

- *Percussion:*

  Percussion is used to assess the size and shape of internal organs and tissue in addition to the assessment of underlying structures, in terms of its solidity, regularity/irregularity, and the presence or absence of fluid and air, for example.

Flatness is normally assessed over muscles and bones, resonance is a hollow sound that is heard, for example, over the air filled lungs, and hyper-resonance is a booming sound that is heard over abnormal lung tissue, as occurs among patients with chronic obstructive pulmonary disease (COPD). Tympany is heard over the stomach with air as a drum like sound, and dullness is normally heard over solid organs, such as the spleen, heart and liver. It is a thud-like sound.

- *Auscultation:*

Using a stethoscope, the diabetes educator listens to the sounds that are produced in the body. The four types of sound that are auscultated are pitch, duration, intensity and quality.

Pitch is the frequency of vibrations. The pitch can be high pitched or low pitched. Duration is the length of time from the beginning to the end of the sound; and intensity is characterized along a continuum from softness to loudness. Lastly, subjective or quality sound characteristics can include such things as irregularity, regularity, grating, booming and other characteristics.

The General Survey

The general survey is an overall look at the patient, their appearance and general state of health.

Some of the things that you can assess as part of the general survey include:

- Weight, height and body build
- Posture, gait, and balance
- Hygiene and grooming
- The person's actual age as compared to their appearance and how old they appear
- Oral and bodily odors
- Signs of distress and/or obvious signs of illness or deformity, such as dyspnea (difficulty breathing), shortness of breath, chest pain and swelling

Height and Weight

The height of the patient can be determined by using the height measurement stick on a standard hospital scale or marking the wall with a strike at the top of the person's head and then using a measuring tape or yardstick to measure the distance from the floor to the mark on the wall.

Weight is assessed using a scale. In order to accurately determine weight loss and weight gain, the patient should be weighed at the same time of the day and wearing the same amount of clothing. When a drastic weight gain occurs, it is possible that the diabetic patient is retaining water from kidney, or renal, complications rather than gaining body weight.

Simply stated, obesity occurs when energy consumed (calories) exceeds energy expended. According to the Centers for Disease Control and Prevention, obesity and overweightness are defined as a high body mass index or BMI. The body mass index is calculated using the person's weight and height; adults with a BMI of less than 25 are not obese or overweight. A BMI of 25 to 29.9 is overweight, and adults with a BMI greater than 30 are considered obese. Though BMI is not a specific indicator of health, as it does not take into account genetics, bone structure, density and weight, or muscle mass, it is a useful tool for a plurality of patients.

The body mass index is calculated by dividing the weight of the patient by the height of the patient in terms of meters squared. For example, if the patient weighs 70 kg, or 154 pounds, and the patient is 165 cm or 1.65 m, the BMI is determined as follows.

70 divided by 1.65

70/2.72 = 25.73

This patient's BMI is 25.73

A large variety of health consequences and illnesses can occur as the result of obesity and overweightness. For example, arthritis, cerebrovascular accidents, cardiovascular disease, diabetes, some forms of cancer like colon cancer and breast cancer, sleep apnea, and other disorders that are related to liver and biliary functioning can occur as the result of obesity.

Vital Signs

The vital signs include the assessment of the pulse, body temperature, respirations, and blood pressure.

- *Pulses*

  Pulse can be assessed at a number of sites including the apical area, using a stethoscope, near the radius, the temporal area of the head, the carotid area of the neck, in the groin area (femoral), the lower legs behind the knee (popliteal), on the inner aspect of the arm in the brachial area, on the front of the foot (dorsalis pedis) and near the ankle (posterior tibial), using the index and middle fingers.

  Pulses are assessed for rate, volume, intensity, rhythm, and bilateral equality. The normal pulse for an adult is from 80 to 100 beats per minute.

  Diabetic patients often have impairments of the pulses and circulation to the lower extremities (the legs and feet). Coolness is an indication of poor circulatory function

71

to the lower extremities; weak dorsalis pedis and posterior tibial pulses also indicate circulatory impairment.

- *Temperature*

Bodily temperature results from the differences between heat production and heat los. The normal oral bodily temperature is 98.6 degrees Fahrenheit, or 36.7 to 37 degrees Centigrade. Temperature can be taken at a number of sites including the mouth, rectum, ear and axillae.

- *Respirations*

Respiratory rate is the only vital sign that humans have some conscious control over, at least until the point when carbon dioxide builds up in the body and one is forced to breathe.

Respirations are assessed, and documented, in terms of rate, regularity, depth and quality, which can include some assessment findings like respiratory stridor, dyspnea, and shortness of breath.

Stridor is respiratory struggling when the patient attempts to breathe using their accessory muscles of respiration; it is most commonly caused by a blockage in the larynx or voice box. It sounds like a high-pitched wheezing noise, and is noticed most when the patient is breathing in, or inhaling, but in some situations it can also be heard when exhaling. Dyspnea is difficult and labored breathing. Any patient with dyspnea or stridor must be given immediate medical attention.

- *Blood Pressure*

Blood pressure results from the pressure of the blood flow as it moves through the arteries. The systolic blood pressure indicates the amount of pressure exerted on the arteries during the heart's contractions; and the diastolic blood pressure indicates the pressure exerted on the arteries when the heart is at rest. Blood pressure is most often measured over the upper arm just above the antecubital space although it can also be measured on other sites such as the legs.

Assessing the Integumentary System

The integumentary system consists of the hair, skin, fingernails and toenails. The diabetic's finger nails and toenails are assessed in terms of texture, blanching and shape (curvature and angle). The skin around the nails is also observed, as well as the color of the nail beds. Diabetic patients may have evidence of poor microcirculation to their feet, as evidence by the loss of the patient's toenails.

The skin is assessed with inspection and palpation and the components of this assessment include the skin's color, moisture, turgor, temperature, and the presence of any edema and/or skin lesions. Skin lesions can lead to severe infections among diabetic patients because their healing process is complicated with the disease.

During the skin assessment the diabetes educator should assess the patient's blood glucose monitoring sites and insulin injection sites for any bruising and hardening.

Assessing the Eyes and Vision

The diabetes educator can visually inspect the conjunctiva, the lacrimal glands and ducts, the clarity of the corneas, the eyelashes, eyebrows, eyebrow movement, eye movement, blinking, and the pupils for size and symmetry. Visual acuity is assessed using the Snellen chart. Diabetic patients often have impaired vision as the result of diabetic retinopathy.

The eyes are also inspected for any signs of infection and irritation, such as discharge and redness. All infections, including eye infections, pose risks among patients affected with diabetes.

ASSESSING LABORATORY AND PATIENT DATA

Blood Glucose Levels

The assessment of blood glucose levels includes self-monitoring and laboratory monitoring.

Those with diabetes perform self-testing of their blood sugar, or blood glucose, levels in order to manage their treatment plan, to prevent long-term complications of diabetes, and to determine if regular insulin is needed before a meal according to their ordered sliding scale.

For example, the patient may have to take 2 units of insulin before their meal if their blood glucose level at that time is from 180 to 220. Only a small drop of blood is necessary for an at-home electronic blood glucose monitoring device.

Useful information needs to be provided to the patient when they self-monitor their blood glucose levels in order to help them judge how well they are doing in terms of achieving their treatment goals. That information may include:

- Information that helps the patient understand how diet and exercise affect blood sugar levels

- Information that helps the patient understand how other factors, such as illness, infection and stress, affect blood sugar levels

- Information that enables the patient to monitor the effect of diabetes medications on blood sugar levels

- Information that enables the patient to identify blood sugar levels that are dangerously high or low so that immediate action(s) can be undertaken.

Blood glucose testing frequency depends greatly on the type of diabetes the patient has and the degree of control that they have. For example, a poorly controlled diabetic patient will have to check their blood glucose levels more often than those who have a pattern of good control. A newly diagnosed diabetic patient may have to monitor their blood glucose levels more often than those who have diabetes for a longer period of time, because the newly diagnosed patient may not immediately have the close balance of medication, diet and exercise that is established and predictable. Adjustments may still be necessary.

Blood glucose monitoring is an essential part of diabetes management. Self-testing is performed with the use of a blood glucose meter, which is a portable electronic device that determines the patient's sugar levels through a small drop of their blood.

The diabetes educator, in collaboration with the healthcare team, will set a target blood glucose range for the patient that is based on a number of factors. These include the patient's overall level of health, the presence of other medical conditions, the patient's age, the type and severity of diabetes, the duration of the disease, the presence of any complications, and the patient's pregnancy status.

An average target range before meals is between 70 and 130 mg/dL; one or two hours after a meal the average target range is lower than 180 mg/dL; and, after fasting, for a minimum of eight hours, the target range averages between 70 and 100 mg/dL.

Fasting Blood Sugar (FBS)

This test is used to diagnosis, confirm and to monitor the success of the established treatment plan for the patient who is affected with diabetes. The normal parameters for a fasting blood sugar level are from 70 to 100 mg/dL.

Oral Glucose Tolerance Test (OGTT)

This test is performed in order to accurately diagnose diabetes mellitus when prior fasting blood sugar tests are either increased or inconsistent.

The patient consumes 75 to 100 grams of glucose after which blood and urine samples are taken immediately and after 30, 60, and 120 minutes of duration after the glucose drink. In some cases, it may also be taken 6 hours after the diagnostic glucose is administered.

The normal parameter for the immediate serum glucose level is between 70 and 110 mg/dL and 60 to 100 mg/dL in the blood. At 30 minutes, the serum levels should be less than 160 mg/dL and the blood levels should be less than 150 mg/dL. At one hour the serum level should be less than 170 mg/dL and the blood should be less than 160 mg/dL. After 2 hours the serum levels should be less than 125 mg/dL and blood level should be less than 115 mg/dL. Lastly, at 3 hours both levels should return to fasting levels.

Values over these normal parameters are indicative of diabetes.

Glycosylated Hemoglobin (Hb A,C)

An A1C blood test, also known as glycated hemoglobin, glycosylated hemoglobin, hemoglobin A1C, and HbA1c, can be used for both diagnosing diabetes and determining how the already diagnosed patient's treatment plan is working. It measures the percentage of hemoglobin, which is a protein in red blood cells that carries oxygen, and is coated with sugar, or glycated.

When used as a diagnostic test, an A1C level of 6.5 or higher indicates diabetes, and if the level is between 5.7 and 6.4 the patient is considered to have prediabetes.

When this test is used to determine the effectiveness of diabetes mellitus treatment, and the level is elevated it indicates an increased risk for complications and that fact that the patient's diabetes mellitus is not being controlled. This test determines how well the patient's blood sugar level has been controlled for the last two to three months. The higher a patient's A1C level, the poorer their blood sugar control is and the greater the A1C, the greater the risk for complications from diabetes.

Lipid Levels

Lipid levels indicate the patient's level of lipids, or fats, that are in the blood. These levels include cholesterol and triglyceride levels. Lipid profiles can be affected by age, gender, genetics, preexisting medical conditions and lifestyle choices including diet, cigarette smoking, consumption patterns, and physical activity levels.

Patients with type 1 diabetes, with controlled blood glucose levels, tend to have lipid levels that can be similar to those without diabetes. In some cases they may even have levels of HDL that are higher than those without diabetes because of the effects of the patient's insulin administration.

Patients who have type 2 diabetes tend to have LDL levels that are similar to those without diabetes, although type 2 diabetic patients tend to have lower HDL levels and higher levels of triglycerides, than those without diabetes. The LDL particles of these patients seem to be smaller and more prone to causing damage than those without diabetes.

Low-risk cholesterol levels in adults with diabetes are LDL levels that are less than 100 mg/dL, HDL levels above 40 mg/dL (women above 50 mg/dL) and triglycerides below 150 mg/dL, according to the American Diabetes Association.

Renal Function

Renal, or kidney, functioning is tested in a number of different ways. Relatively simple blood tests measure the blood's levels, such as urea and creatinine. Urea and creatinine are waste products in the blood; higher levels of these waste products in the blood indicate that the kidneys are not effectively and efficiently getting rid of them.

Urine testing can also reveal abnormalities of renal functioning and chronic kidney failure; and diagnostic imaging tests, like ultrasound tests, can assess the patient's kidney structure, size and the degree that the kidneys are affected using sound waves or echogenicity. The last form of kidney function test is biopsy, which allows a small sample of kidney tissue to be examined to help determine the cause for a kidney problem(s).

Liver Function

Liver function tests are blood tests that measure the levels of certain enzymes and proteins in the patient's blood. These tests are used to diagnose and monitor liver function and liver disease. For example, liver function tests can screen for liver infectious diseases like hepatitis; they monitor the progression of an existing disease, such as alcoholic cirrhosis and viral hepatitis to determine how well the treatment is working; they measure the severity of a liver disease; and they can also monitor for side effects of medications that can be hepatotoxic.

When tests of liver function are too high or low, it indicates poor liver function.

Examples of common liver function tests are as follows:

- *Albumin and total protein.* Albumin is needed to help fight infections and perform other liver functions. Lower than normal albumin indicates liver damage or disease.

- *Bilirubin.* Bilirubin is produced when red blood cells break down, and it passes through the liver and is excreted in the stool. Elevated levels indicate liver damage and disease and it can also be observed with the presence of jaundice.

- *L-lacatate dehydrogenase (LD).* LD is an enzyme that is found in the liver, and when the levels are elevated, it can indicate liver damage.

- *SGOT.* This test monitors the amount of glutamic-oxaloacetic transaminase in the blood. This enzyme is found in the liver, muscles and red blood cells.

Insulin Pumps

An insulin pump can be used instead of insulin injections. Insulin pumps are most commonly used for patients of all ages with Type 1 diabetes, although now, it is becoming increasingly more commonly used among patients with Type 2 diabetes as well.

The diabetes educator, in collaboration with the patient's physician and other members of the healthcare team, can decide if an insulin pump is appropriate for the patient.

Insulin pumps deliver insulin on a 24-hour basis throughout the day. Insulin is delivered through a catheter under the patient's skin. The insulin delivery can be a basal rate of insulin, a bolus dose of insulin, and a supplemental dose of insulin

The basal insulin dose keeps the patient's blood glucose level within target range between meals and overnight over a 24-hour period of time. Different amounts of insulin are often programmed at different times throughout the day and night.

Bolus insulin is delivered while the patient is eating. This type of insulin covers carbohydrates in the patient's meal and it can be adjusted depending on the patient's consumption. Lastly, supplemental and corrective boluses of insulin can be delivered with an insulin pump when the patient is affected with high blood glucose levels.

Data Patterns and Trends

All patient data is highly useful for monitoring the patient and the success of their treatment plan. When data is collected and aggregated over time, patterns and trends can be quite easily analyzed and identified.

For example, the patient data may show an increase, or decrease, of diabetes control over time. It could also be noted that blood glucose levels are higher on Saturdays and Sundays than those taken during the week, for example. This analysis showed a pattern of noncompliance with the diet on weekends. The diabetes educator should explore this pattern with the patient in order to find a way that weekend dietary management can be successful.

III. ASSESSING KNOWLEDGE AND PRACTICES

KNOWLEDGE AND SKILLS

Simply stated, entry-level knowledge and skills is defined as baseline knowledge and skills. The diabetes educator assesses and determines the patient's entry-level knowledge and skills in order to plan appropriate educational activities to meet the patient's educational needs.

Entry level knowledge and skills consists of what the patient knows at the current time and what the patient can do at the current time, respectively. After this determination, the diabetes educator compares this entry-level knowledge and skills to what the patient should know and what they should be able to do. This comparison is used to determine specific learning needs for the patient.

The learning need = what the patient should know MINUS what the patient actually knows now (cognitive domain entry level)

The learning need = what the patient should be able to do MINUS what the patient can actually do now (psychomotor domain entry level)

The assessment of entry-level knowledge and skills also gives the diabetes educator the opportunity to identify any false knowledge, misinformation and poor self-management skills. Again, the diabetes educator with planned educational activities can address these deficits.

Intermediate Knowledge and Habits

The diabetic patient should be fully knowledgeable about:

- The types of diabetes
- The diagnosis, signs and symptoms of diabetes
- Diabetes medications
- The interrelationships of diet, exercise and medications
- The prevention of complications
- Monitoring techniques and equipment
- The short term complications of diabetes like hypoglycemia
- The long term complications of diabetes like retinopathy

The diabetes educator should assess entry-level knowledge in all of the above knowledge and skills and then plan appropriate educational activities specific to the patient's needs that moves them to higher levels within the cognitive and psychomotor domains of learning.

Nutritional Habits

The diabetes educator also assesses the patient and significant other's entry-level knowledge in terms of diet as well as their dietary habits, which may or may not be the habits that the patient should have.

For example, some diabetic patients do not follow their dietary regime because they are just simply not compliant and they choose not to follow the plan, whereas other diabetic patients may not eat the proper diet because they have a knowledge deficit.

The diabetes educator can help both the patient who lacks knowledge about the diabetic diet and the patient who is not compliant with their dietary regime. The noncompliant patient can be assisted to become compliant when the diabetes educator employs some of the principles described above in terms of motivation and change theories. The patient who is not following the diet as a result of a knowledge deficit can be helped by the diabetes educator with planned educational activities to meet this educational need.

A good way to determine what the patient typically eats is to ask the patient what they had for breakfast, lunch, dinner and snacks during the previous 24 hours.

Some dietary specific areas that should be included in the assessment include food and beverage choices, portion sizes, and the timing of meals and snacks. Specific recommendations according to the American Diabetics Association are explained below.

Exercise and Levels of Physical Activity

- **Types of Exercise**

  The types of exercise are classified according to the type of muscle contraction. For example, there are isotonic, isometric or isokinetic exercises; other classifications include aerobic and anaerobic exercises.

  Isotonic exercises, also referred to as dynamic exercises, are exercises that produce muscle contraction and active movement with muscle shortening. Examples of isotonic exercises are running, walking, swimming, physical conditioning exercises, performing the activities of daily living (ADLs) and performing active ROM exercises.

  This type of exercise increases strength, muscle tone and mass and it also helps to maintain joint flexibility and enhance circulation. Blood flow is increased to all body parts during this type of exercise because heart rate speeds up and the cardiac output increases.

  Isometric exercises, also known as static or setting exercises, include no joint movement and the muscle length does not change with muscle contraction. These exercises focus on strengthening gluteal, quadriceps and abdominal muscles, increasing endurance and increasing muscular strength.

Isokinetic exercises, also known as resistive exercises, are exercises that are done against resistance, which causes muscle contraction and muscular tension. These exercises can help to build up certain muscle groups and increase blood pressure and blood flow. Special machines and devices provide the resistance necessary for a patient to perform these exercises.

Aerobic exercises are exercises with which the body takes in more oxygen than is needed to actually perform the exercise. These exercises help improve cardiovascular conditioning as well as physical fitness.

Anaerobic exercises are exercises, like endurance training, where the anaerobic pathways are needed to provide additional energy because the muscles are not able to draw enough oxygen from the bloodstream alone.

- **The Benefits of Exercise**

  Exercise is required to help all people maintain good physical and mental health. Exercise benefits the different systems in the body in a variety of ways.

  o The musculoskeletal system benefits with mild to strenuous exercise. The size, strength, shape and tone of muscles are all maintained through exercise. Joints receive nourishment, flexibility, stability and range of motion through exercise. Weight bearing is needed to maintain strength and bone density as well.

  o The cardiovascular system is also benefited through physical activity and exercise. Physical activity has been shown to help prevent strokes and cardiovascular disease. Exercise, such as walking a mile in fifteen to twenty minutes, increases the heart rate, and the strength of heart's muscle contraction. Increased cardiac output occurs, because this type of exercise increases the blood supply to the heart and muscles. Aerobic exercise and yoga, in particular, have been shown to produce highly beneficial cardiac benefits.

  o The respiratory system has its own benefits from exercise. Gas exchange is improved through the ventilation and oxygenation that occurs during exercise. Deep breaths during exercise help to release toxins and the increased oxygen to the brain helps cognitive functioning and emotional stability. Exercising regularly and paying attention to deep breathing can help to improve one's stamina, through oxygenation.

  o The immune system functioning is also improved through exercise, because there is increased circulation to the lymph system. Moderate exercise enhances immunity, but a pattern of strenuous exercise can reduce immune function.

Moderate exercise has been shown to benefit circulating T-cell function and cytokine production. These changes enhance the body's resistance to viral infections and it prevents the formation of malignant cells within the body.

o The benefits of exercise for the gastrointestinal system include an increase in appetite, increased gastrointestinal tract tone and enhanced peristalsis. Performing abdominal exercises, such as rowing, walking, swimming and doing sit-ups, can relieve constipation. These types of exercises can also help with irritable bowel syndrome and other digestive disorders.

o Exercising helps the metabolic/endocrine system, through the elevation of the metabolic rate, which, in turn, then increases body heat, waste product removal, and calorie elimination. The increase of metabolic rate can last even after the exercise is completed. Blood sugar can be stabilized and the cells can become more responsive to insulin with weight loss and exercise. Cholesterol levels and the levels of serum triglycerides are reduced as a result of the increased use of triglycerides and fatty acids that occurs during exercise.

o Exercise also helps the urinary system because it promotes efficient blood flow and it allows the body to excrete wastes more efficiently. The risk of urinary tract infections also decreases with exercise, because exercise prevents the stasis of urine in the bladder.

o The psycho-neurologic system can be positively affected with exercise. Exercise can help elevate one's mood and it can also help to relieve stress and anxiety. Symptoms of depression can be relieved through both aerobic and anaerobic exercises, because there is an increased production of serotonin and norepinephrine in the person's body. The increase of endorphins and the increased level of oxygen to the brain and other bodily systems induces euphoria. Additionally, stress can be released through muscular exertion.

o Exercise helps cognitive functioning as well as spiritual health. This can be beneficial to patients with ADHD or ADD, by increasing their ability to problem solve, pay attention and plan. Exercise has also been shown to strengthen cells in the brain, which helps a person affected with mood problems in terms of learning and problem solving. Yoga and meditation have also been shown to help with relaxation and concentration.

Internal Factors That Affect Exercise and Activity

- *Growth and Development*

Posture, body proportions, body mass, body movements and reflexes are all affected by a person's age and the development of their musculoskeletal system and nervous system. Movements in a newborn are reflexive and random, but as the neurological system matures, this changes.

During the first year, control over movement progresses and changes start to occur. Before fine motor skills are developed, gross motor development occurs. This development occurs starting with head control and movement, to crawling, pulling up to a standing position, to standing and then walking. Walking generally occurs between twelve to fifteen months of age.

Gross and fine motor skills, such as running, jumping, using crayons, zippering and tooth brushing, are refined from one to five years old. The refinement of motor skills continues from six to twelve years old, and the exercise patterns for the rest of their life are usually also determined at this age. During the adolescent years, changes to posture can occur as a result of growth spurts and life-related factors such as computer use and carrying heavy book bags.

There are usually very few physical changes that affect mobility in adults from the age of twenty to forty, except for the changes that occur with pregnancy. During pregnancy the center of gravity is altered which can affect the pregnant woman's center of gravity and their balance. Exercise has proven to be helpful for pregnant women, but they should always consult their physician before beginning an exercise routine. Gestational diabetes, even in obese women, can be prevented by exercise; and it can also benefit pregnant women with their ability to lose weight after they deliver.

Muscle tone and bone density tend to decrease, as a person grows older; and reaction times tend to slow as well. Other things that generally occur among the members of the aging population are a decrease in joint flexibility, and a decrease in bone mass, particularly seen in women with osteoporosis. Osteoporosis affects mostly the weight bearing joints in the lower extremities and the anterior aspects of the spinal bones. This spinal involvement can cause compression fractures to the vertebrae; lower joint and back osteoporosis can lead to hip fractures. Posture, gait and balance are affected in many older adults as a result of these changes.

- *Nutritional Status*

Body alignment and mobility can be affected among over and under nourished people. Obesity can affect posture, balance and joint health as the result of distorted movement and stress on joints. Under nourished people can experience muscle weakness and fatigue, and if their vitamin D level is low, bone deformity during growth can occur. Osteoporosis can become a risk factor with a vitamin D and calcium deficiency. Vitamin D and calcium should be supplemented among postmenopausal women who are at great risk for osteoporosis.

- *Personal Values and Attitudes*

Family influences can affect the amount of exercise a person participates in. If a family actively participates in physical activity, then generally their children tend to do so as well. For example, children of those who participated in, or still participate in, sports are more likely to participate as well.

- *Values*

  Personal values also influence a person's choice of physical activity or type of exercise. A person's choice can vary depending on geographic location and cultural expectations. If exercise is looked at negatively, such as a chore that must be done, this may decrease one's desire to participate, whereas if it is looked at as a bettering of one's health and an overall essential part of self-care, it is a more likely choice and one that can be enjoyed by the patient.

The FIT model of exercise includes an individualized exercise program in terms of the frequency of the activity, the intensity of the exercise and time spent exercising. This model allows a person to have a tailored exercise routine made just for them. These parameters can change over time as the patient's impacting factors improve or decrease. For example, a patient who is recovering from a below the knee amputation will have a routine that begins with easier movements and then progresses to optimal full movement and strength.

It is important to find individualized motivating factors that can help the patient to achieve their exercise goals and also to allow them to experience some pleasure while exercising. For example, a patient can be motivated to meet their goals through the use of music, an exercise partner, a challenge, keeping a daily log to show their progression, etc. Each patient's routine varies depending on their age, illness, injury or disorder, and other factors.

External Factors That Affect Exercise and Activity

External factors, such as temperature and humidity, can affect a person's mobility and exercise. If the temperature or humidity is at a level that is uncomfortable for a patient, this tends to deter them from wanting to participate; whereas if the temperature is at a comfortable level and the humidity is low a patient may be more prone to participate.

Other external factors can include the availability, and non-accessibility, of recreational facilities, which can be lacking because of the patient's financial inability to attend an indoor recreational or gym facility.

Prescribed Limitations

In some situations, there are medical limitations to mobility that are necessary. Some disorders and diseases have side effects that limit the patient's ability to exercise. For example, if a patient experiences shortness of breath they may not be able to participate in much cardiovascular exercise. Patients who just had surgery for a limb amputation may be limited in regards to physical activity and movement.

Assistive Devices

Assistive devices are available to patients that are in need of extra help with mobility. A cane is one of these assistive devices. There are three types of canes. The standard cane, which has one foot, the tripod cane, which has three feet, and the quad cane, which has four feet.

Rubber caps are placed on the cane tips to help prevent the patient from slipping and to improve traction. The proper length cane allows for the elbow of the patient to be only slightly flexed. Depending on the amount of support necessary, the patient can use one or two canes.

Walkers are assistive devices that are used by patients who require more support than a cane. There are different sizes of walkers available to fit the needs of patients. It is important that the walker be properly fitted for each patient prior to use. Some walkers require that the patient pick it up to move, whereas others are available with two or four wheels. The wheeled walkers do not require the patient to lift them, but they are not as stable as a standard walker. Added features can include a seat and brakes.

A wheelchair is another assistive device that may be used by patients to aid in mobility. Anytime a patient is in a wheelchair safety precautions must be taken. The foot pedals of the wheelchair must be raised before helping the patient into the chair. The brakes on both wheels of the chair should be locked when the chair is not in motion. There is a seatbelt on the chair to aid in extra support for the patient. The chair should always be backed into an elevator and, if there is an incline, the person pushing the chair should be between the incline and the chair.

Monitoring Techniques and Equipment

Like other entry-level knowledge and skills, the diabetes educator assesses how well the patient is able to measure their blood glucose levels and ketones. This assessment can be done by asking the patient to perform both skills as you observe them. You will then determine exactly which skills, and aspects of these tasks, need correction and patient education.

The patient's performance should be compared and contrasted to standard procedures in order to determine the patient's learning needs.

Record-Keeping Activities

Examining the documentation that the patient has recorded over time can assess the patient's record keeping.

Some of these record-keeping activities include blood glucose levels, dietary intake, medications taken, and levels of activity. Blood glucose levels should be taken and recorded in a logbook that is often included with the blood glucose monitoring packaging.

These blood glucose levels, in combination with levels of activity, medications taken, including regular insulin coverage, and dietary intake provide the doctor and the diabetes educator with the data necessary to determine patterns, trends, and the interrelationships of blood glucose levels, diet, medication and exercise, as specific to the patient.

MEDICATION ADMINISTRATION

Medication administration skills and abilities are assessed by asking the patient to perform tasks, such as the self-administration of oral and injectable medications and their techniques, the use of delivery systems, and the timing, dosage of medication and adherence to the patient's medication regimen.

Drawing the Insulin Dose From the Bottle

The following is the standard procedure for drawing up insulin dosages from the bottle. This procedure should be used by the diabetes educator for both teaching and for assessing the patient's technique.

1. Wash hands thoroughly
2. Mix the insulin the solution by gently rotating the bottle between the palms of the hands. It should NOT be shaken since this will cause bubbles that are difficult to get rid of.
3. The protective cap of the vial is removed when the first dose of the new bottle is being drawn up or the rubber top of a vial should be cleaned with alcohol if the vial has already been opened.
4. Remove the cap of the needle
5. Draw up the amount of air that equals the dose of the insulin that is needed
6. Insert the needle into the center of the rubber cap and inject the air
7. Draw up the correct insulin dosage without taking the needle out of the bottle
8. The dose is checked by holding the needle at eye level. The correct dose is the ordered number of units of insulin PLUS 0.25 units to clear the syringe during injection
9. The needle should be tapped to dislodge any air bubbles when necessary
10. Discard the needle and syringe in the proper container.

Mixing Insulin

The following is the standard procedure for drawing up mixed insulin dosages. This procedure should also be used by the diabetes educator for both teaching and for assessing the patient's technique.

1. Inject the amount of air that is equal to the long acting NPH insulin dosage into the NPH bottle without letting the tip of the needle touch the insulin in the bottle
2. Remove the needle
3. Inject the amount of air that is equal to the regular insulin dosage into the regular insulin bottle
4. Draw up the regular insulin dosage without removing the needle after injecting the air
5. Reinsert the needle with the regular insulin into the NPH vial bottle
6. Draw up the correct NPH dosage

7. If an incorrect NPH dosage was drawn up, it is necessary to discard all of the insulin and begin the process again using a new needle.
8. Discard the needle and syringe in the proper container.

Subcutaneous Injection

Subcutaneous injections can be given in the abdomen, upper arms and the front of the thighs. The correct procedure that the patient should be taught about is as follows:

1. Select the site.
2. Clean the injection site with an alcohol swab in an outward circular pattern of about 2 inches.
3. Gently pinch the site so a 1-inch fat fold appears.
4. Position the needle with the bevel up and insert it at a 45-degree angle unless you CANNOT pinch an inch or more. In this case, use a 90-degree angle.
5. Release the skin pinch.
6. Pull the plunger back to check for blood. If blood appears withdraw the needle and start again.
7. Slowly inject the medication.
8. Withdraw the needle and cover the site with an alcohol swab.
9. Gently massage the site.
10. Discard the needle and syringe in the proper container.

HEALTH CARE RESOURCES

Health Care Professionals

Diabetic patients often need a complete team of healthcare professionals that can coordinate and collaborate in order to optimally meet all the bio-psycho-social needs of the patient and significant others.

Many patients may not be aware of these healthcare resources so the diabetes educator must assess the patient's knowledge about these resources and plan teaching according to this assessment so the patient can maximize these resources.

The Roles of Medical and Allied Health Professionals

- *Medical Professionals*

  There are a wide variety of medical doctors who perform different roles and who have specialty areas of practice. For example, diabetic patients should have a primary care physician; others also have a specialist, such as an endocrinologist and/or nephrologist when they have renal alterations as the result of their diabetes.

  Other medical roles include those provided by doctors of osteopathy (DO) and doctors of chiropractic medicine. Additionally, there are medical physician extenders like physician assistants and nurse practitioners who perform limited roles in all types of healthcare settings and in all levels of care.

- *The Nurse*

  Nurses play a pivotal role in the assessing, planning, implementing and evaluating the care of the patient in collaboration with the other members of the healthcare team, including the diabetes educator.

  In many settings, throughout the 24 hours of each day, nursing is the only healthcare member that is present or on call.

- *Restorative and Rehabilitation Services*

  Physical, occupational and speech therapists are also a part of the healthcare team when patients are in need of restorative and/or rehabilitation care. The goals of restorative and rehabilitation care include increasing the patient's physical strength to offset physical limitations. Some of these rehabilitative treatments include assistance with transfers, gait, balance and ambulation, as are often necessary when the patient has peripheral neuropathy, has had a cerebrovascular accident or has just gotten a prosthesis.

Restorative and rehabilitation care also aims to maintain and enhance the patient's level of independence, which increases their self-worth, self-esteem, self-control and quality of life. Correcting swallowing disorders and oral communication impairments, with the help of a speech and language therapist, are also needed when the diabetic patient has been affected with a cerebrovascular accident, or stroke, as a complication of their diabetes.

- *The Physiotherapist*

In a collaborative assessment process, the physiotherapist evaluates the patient's physical capabilities and limitations. Physiotherapists administer therapies that are designed to correct or minimize deformity, increase mobility and strength or alleviate discomfort or pain. Specific exercises, such as heat, cold, aqua therapy or electro-physical therapy may be ordered and used to treat the patient.

- *The Physical Therapist*

Physical therapists assess, plan, implement and evaluate interventions including those related to strength, mobility, balance, gait, coordination and range of motion. At times, the physical therapist may have the assistance of physical therapy assistants or physical therapy aides.

- *The Occupational Therapist*

Occupational therapists assess, plan, implement and evaluate interventions including those that assist patients to achieve their highest possible level of independence in terms of the patient's activities of daily living.

They assess the need for and provide the patient with adaptive devices like special cutlery to facilitate independent eating, long shoe horns so the patient can put their shoes on without bending over, special grasping tools to facilitate the patient's ability to pick items up from the floor, and special devices to manipulate buttoning so the person can dress themselves independently.

In preparation for transition back into the community, the occupational therapist may even go out and assess the patient's home to ensure that the home environment is both safe and conducive to the patient's independence level. At times, the occupational therapist will recommend, and arrange for, some home modifications and equipment that may be necessary to increase the patient's independent function. For example, ramps, wheelchair lifts, and the installation of handrails in the shower may be necessary and indicated. Occupational therapists may also have the assistance of an occupational therapy assistants or aides.

- *The Speech Pathologist/Therapist*

  Speech pathologist/therapists assess, diagnose and treat any communication disorders and swallowing disorders (dysphagia). For example, a speech therapist may help the patient to form words when the patient is affected with expressive aphasia as often occurs after a stroke. They may employ assistive devices like word boards, and they actively collaborate with the dietician in terms of nutrition when the patient that has a swallowing disorder which can lead to aspiratory and respiratory compromise.

- *Respiratory Therapists*

  Respiratory therapists perform a number of different things, including collaborative patient assessment and planning, diagnostic procedures like drawing arterial blood gas specimens, and the provision of care, including managing respiratory treatments like nebulizers, CPAP and BPAP, setting up and maintaining mechanical ventilation, assisting the patient with respiratory exercises and the administration of respiratory related medications and drugs.

  Many diabetic patients with severe complications require the services of respiratory therapists.

- *Social Workers*

  Social workers counsel and assist patients, as well as their families, who are experiencing personal problems as a result of injury or illness. By liaising with existing community groups and resources, a social worker acts as a patient advocate. They also assist the patient along with their family, to deal with issues having to do with the illness or condition, such as any social, domestic, financial and emotional implications they may have.

- *The Dietician*

  The dietician works closely with the patient and the diabetes educator in terms of assessing, planning implementing and evaluation dietary related patient education; and they also plan an appropriate diet for diabetic patients as based on their assessed needs, patient preferences and other factors.

- *The Podiatrist*

  Podiatrists often work with diabetic patients because diabetes often adversely affects the foot. The podiatrist assesses the patient's feet, prevents foot complications and also treats any foot disorders within their scope of practice.

The podiatrist plays an important role in maintaining the health as well as the integrity of the patient's feet and toenails. The feet of the patient with diabetes must be in good condition. For example, there should be no nail disorders or skin lesions.

Appropriate footwear for the patient is also very essential, so they work closely with the patient and their caregiver to select the appropriate footwear for them.

- *The Prosthetist/Orthotist*

Assessing the need for prosthesis, such as an artificial limb, is the responsibility of the prosthetists. Once the prosthetist has performed an assessment of the patient, they will then design and supply the patient with any necessary prosthesis. Typically, a patient will get a trial temporary prosthesis before they are fitted with a permanent one.

The prosthetist can also modify an existing prosthesis to meet the patient's needs as well as checking on the patient at regular intervals to make sure that the prosthesis is working properly, comfortable and meeting the patient's needs.

Mechanical devices such as splints or braces for the neck, arm or leg, which are known as orthoses, are used in order to correct deformities that the patient may have. Orthotists provide these devices and they also provide some added support to the patient.

- *The Psychiatrist and Psychologist*

A psychiatrist or psychologist will be involved in the caring process if the patient is experiencing a psychiatric or emotional problem as the result of the diabetes and/or the complications associated with it.

- *The Case Manager*

A relatively new member of the healthcare team is the case manager. When case managers are part of the healthcare team, which is not always the case, the case manager's responsibility is to develop a formal, written comprehensive needs assessment, which includes a formal review of all the evaluations that are performed by all the other team members.

The elements or components of case management include:

- Linking diabetic patients to the services that they need. For example, the case manager may facilitate the services of a physical therapist or podiatrist
- Coordinating and evaluating the timeliness, effectiveness and appropriateness of care
- Identifying any deviations from the plan of care and poor outcomes and then correcting these problems

- Ensuring that the patient is at, or moved to, the appropriate level of care so insurance reimbursement for services is possible

Health Insurance

Diabetes educators, in collaboration with other members of the healthcare team, not only insure that good care is provided, they must also insure that the care is provided at the appropriate level of care.

Levels of care, along the continuum, from the most intensive to the least intensive include emergency departments and critical care areas, progressive or "step down" acute care areas, acute care areas, subacute and rehabilitation centers, skilled nursing long term care, home care and assisted living, and independent living.

The patient's needed level of care depends on a number of factors including the severity of their disease or disorder, the presence of any complications, the presence of any comorbidities and other factors.

Criteria for admission and discharge from a healthcare facility as well as other levels of care, including homecare, are established by private and governmental agencies. When patients meet admission criteria, the case is accepted and reimbursed for. When a patient does not meet the criteria for admission, the patient is referred to another level of care.

Reimbursement Methodologies

- *Prospective Reimbursement*

  In the past, hospitals were reimbursed for care as based on the services provided. This form of reimbursement was referred to as retrospective reimbursement. In essence, there was no reason to contain costs because insurance payers paid for all services regardless of costs. As healthcare costs continued to spiral, cost containment concerns gave rise to prospective reimbursement.

  With prospective reimbursement, the healthcare organization is reimbursed as based on a fixed rate that is attached to the patient's diagnosis related groups (DRG). Hospitals that are able to provide good care and outcomes with short lengths of stay and limited resources and care make more money than those with prolonged lengths of stay and unlimited resources. Essentially, everything after admission is overhead. Reimbursement is no longer unlimited with prospective reimbursement.

- *Governmental Reimbursement*

  The federal Medicare program and the state-administered Medicaid programs are two primary governmental reimbursement programs. Medicare, under the U. S. Social Security Act, reimburses care for older adults who are 65 years of age and older, permanently disabled people and their dependents.

Medicaid, on the other hand, provides healthcare reimbursement for low-income individuals, families and chronically ill children.

- *Third Party Private Insurance Companies*

    Private insurance companies are numerous. Each differs in terms of monthly premiums, covered services, copayments, deductibles and reimbursement rates. Many corporate businesses use private insurance companies as part of the health benefit that full-time and/or part time employees get.

- *Personal Payment*

    The number of people who are able to directly pay for all healthcare services and hospitalizations are few and far between, especially with the current monumental costs of healthcare and healthcare services.

- *The Uninsured*

    Sadly, there are many people who are uninsured. Some uninsured people may qualify for Medicaid, but others may not. Charities and charitable groups can sometimes assist these insured people.

Supplies and Durable Medical Equipment

Diabetes educators, in collaboration with others, manage medical supplies and durable medical equipment as based on the patient's needs. Medicare, Medicaid and private insurance companies need a justification for the rental or purchase of medical equipment and supplies, such as needles, blood glucose meters, walkers, wheelchairs, prostheses and dialysis supplies and equipment.

The patient's independent practitioner, such as a medical doctor, physician's assistant or nurse practitioner, must submit a Certificate of Medical Necessity. The medical supplies and durable medical equipment will be then be provided, and reimbursed for by the payer, only when this Certificate of Medical Necessity reflects the fulfillment of established criteria for reimbursement.

Support Services and Pharmaceuticals

Like durable medical equipment and supplies, support services and pharmaceuticals are reimbursed only when there is documented medical necessity for these services. Some of the support services that are reimbursed for, as based on actual need, include the services of occupational therapists, speech and language therapists, physical therapists, transportation, medications and home health care.

IV. INTERVENTION

INDIVIDUALIZING EDUCATION PLANS

Learning Objectives and Behavioral Goals

Learning objectives guide the teaching process and enable diabetes educators to objectively evaluate the outcomes and effectiveness of the teaching. Learning objectives are established during the planning phase of the patient and family education process.

Learning objectives must be:

- Learner, not teacher oriented
- Specific
- Measurable and behavioral
- Congruent with the domain and level of knowledge
- Consistent with the assessed need

On the next page are some examples of learning objectives:

Learner Oriented Learning Objective: The learner will be able to describe the components of the diabetic diet.	**Teacher Oriented Learning Objective:** The diabetes educator will instruct the patient about community resources.
Specific Learning Objectives: The learner will be able to list the basic food groups.	**Non-Specific Learning Objectives:** The learner will be able discuss food.
Measurable/ Behavioral Learning Objective: The learner will correctly demonstrate the procedure for the self-administration of insulin.	**Non Measurable & Non Behavioral Learning Objective:** The learner will be able understand insulin.
Objective That is Consistent With The Learning Domain: The learner will be able to demonstrate the proper glucose level monitoring.	**Objective That is NOT Consistent With The Learning Domain:** The learner will be able to describe the proper glucose level monitoring.
Objective That is Consistent With The Level of the Domain: Categorize (synthesis) the degree of risk associated with multiple & complex risk factor relationships (synthesis)	**Objective That is NOT Consistent With The Level of the Domain:** List (knowledge) the degree of risk associated with multiple & complex risk factor relationships (synthesis)

The best way to write learning objectives is to begin with the statement, "*At the conclusion of the teaching, the learner will be able to:*" and then start the statement with a measurable verb that is consistent with the domain of learning and domain level such as those below:

Cognitive Domain:

- Define
- Describe
- Identify
- Discuss
- Name
- List
- State
- Relate
- Apply
- Explain
- Summarize
- Outline

Psychomotor Domain:

- Use
- Perform
- Demonstrate

Affective Domain:

- Demonstrate a belief
- Complies
- Accepts
- Values

Information Sequencing

Generally speaking, content and information should be sequenced from the known to the unknown, from the simple to the complex and from the least threatening to the most threatening.

For example, when the diabetes educator wants to teach about the diabetic diet, the diabetes educator will sequence the content and information to move the patient from information about the basic food groups (simple and known) to the interactions of foods and food choices on the blood glucose levels (complex and unknown). Additionally, when teaching the diabetic patient about the self-injection of insulin, the diabetes educator will allow the patient to practice injection techniques on an orange (less threatening) and then move the patient to insulin injection into their own abdomen (more threatening).

The knowledge, skills and abilities will also be sequenced according to the levels of complexity for each of the domains of learning. The levels of complexity and difficulty for each of the three domains of learning are below.

The Cognitive Domain

There are six levels or categories to the cognitive domain. Arranged from the least complex to the most complex, these six levels are as follows:

- *Knowledge:* This level consists of the simple recall of learned facts.

- *Comprehension:* At this level, the patient is able to get some meaning and understanding of the material presented by the learning activity. The patient has interpreted and comprehended the presented information.

- *Application:* As the learner completes this level of the cognitive domain, the learner is able to use and apply the material that was learned in a new or different situation. For example, the diabetic patient will apply the principles of regular insulin coverage to a situation when their blood glucose levels are elevated (different or new situation).

- *Analysis:* At this level of cognitive sequencing, the learner is able to break down material into smaller parts. This enables one to see relationships among the parts and/or some unifying principles or themes. For example, the diabetic patient will see the relationships among medication, diet and exercise.

- *Synthesis:* The patient is now able to put together parts or pieces of the newly learned knowledge in order to create a new whole concept, a new structure and/or a new pattern. For example, the patient may develop their own sick day plan or a plan for days when the level of exercise is anticipated to be greater than normal.

- *Evaluation:* Evaluation is the highest and most complex level of the cognitive, or knowledge, domain. This level contains elements of the other five, or lower, levels of the cognitive domain in addition to a conscious value judgment based on some objective criteria. For example, the diabetic patient at this highest sequenced level of knowledge will value diabetic self-care.

The Psychomotor Domain

The psychomotor domain, also known as the doing domain, is comprised of "hands on skills". Some examples of this domain are taking a pulse or a blood pressure, walking with crutches, the self administration of insulin using a needle and syringe, and the use of a piece of equipment, such as a blood glucose monitor.

There are seven levels/categories to this domain. These domains are, once again, arranged from the least to the most complex, as follows:

- *Perception:* At this most basic level of the psychomotor domain, the patient is able to sense and perceive relevant cues. An example of this is when a patient observes the diabetes educator's steps for administering their insulin or taking their blood glucose level.

- *Set:* The patient is mentally willing to act and to perform a certain action. An example of this is when the patient is able, and willing, to draw up normal saline, or sterile water, and inject it into an orange, as preparation to more complex and advanced teaching relating to his or her own self injection of insulin.

- *Guided response:* After the demonstration of a skill, the patient will imitate the skill or technique. Initially, the patient's performance is not done with accuracy, confidence or in a proficient manner. An example of someone demonstrating a guided response is when a patient, under the direct guidance of a diabetes educator, injects insulin into his or her own abdomen for the first time.

- *Mechanism:* Mechanism is a proficient, habitual performance of a skill with a decent degree of competence and confidence. An example of a patient performing at this level of the psychomotor domain would be a patient who continues injecting themselves with their own insulin for a period of time.

- *Complex overt response:* The patient's psychomotor skill is now correct, smooth and quick; it is somewhat automatic and coordinated. Competence and confidence continue to grow as the patient continues to perform the learned skill.

- *Adaptation:* Adaptation occurs when the learner is able to modify the psychomotor skill on their own when problems or unusual circumstances arise. An example of this would be when a patient draws up regular insulin, rather than NPH insulin (problem or unusual situation), and they are able to quickly replace the regular insulin into the bottle and then draw up the NPH without discarding the entire dose, needle and syringe.

- *Origination:* At this highest level, the patient is able to create a new pattern of movement so they can overcome a complex problem or a new situation.

The Affective Domain

The affective domain includes the development of attitudes, beliefs, values and opinions. This domain is also known as the feeling domain. An example of affective domain competency is developing a commitment to a lifestyle change. There are five levels, or categories, in this domain, and they are, once again, arranged from the least to the most complex, as follows:

- *Receiving:* This phase of the affective domain involves a simple willingness to hear about particular phenomena or stimuli. For example, a patient may be willing to listen to a short explanation about their responsibilities regarding health and wellness.

- *Responding:* The patient reacts and responds to a particular stimulus or phenomena. It is here that the person may react to their wellness responsibilities.

- *Valuing:* The patient, at this level, is able to attach some worth and value to a thing such as diabetes self-care.

- *Organization:* The individual is now able to resolve conflicts among different forces, to bring together different value systems, and begin to develop their own personally, internally consistent, harmonious value system.

- *Characterization by a value or a value complex:* The patient's value system becomes extremely pervasive, consistent and predictable over time. Throughout the course of their day, they are able to value wellness in a predictable manner and to demonstrate healthy life style choices.

Selecting Content

The content for the educational activity must be consistent with assessed learning needs, the domain of learning and the level of the domain of learning that is appropriate to and consistent with the identified educational needs.

The content should also reflect the fact that learning style and preferences as well as cultural aspects are effectively integrated into the content and materials.

Communication and Modifying Communication and Teaching According to Age-Specific Characteristics and Needs

Although it not always precisely clear and exact where one age category or classification begins and ends, we are somewhat guided by the principles of age group characteristics and needs. Additionally, there can be some variance within age groups having to do with a particular patient's characteristics and needs. For instance, a middle age person can demonstrate the needs and characteristics of an older person and vice-versa.

These age group characteristics are considered a generalized guideline, but each person has to be assessed on a case-to-case basis. Age related characteristics and needs have implications on how we implement patient/family education and how we communicate with the patients.

- *Infants*

An infant is cognitively unable to learn health related information and, obviously, unable to even ask a question, therefore, the obvious focus of the teaching will certainly be the caregiver(s), usually the parent(s).

- *Toddlers*

  Toddlers have a limited ability to learn; they have a short attention span so, for this reason, they should be taught things in short, concrete sentences. Useful teaching aides for the toddler include picture books, dolls, puppets, pictures and stories.

- *School Age Children*

  This age group can benefit from appropriate fun, colorful and exciting books.

- *Adolescents*

  A suitable strategy for motivating an adolescent would be to include them in peer group learning with other patients of similar age and condition.

- *Young and Middle Years Adults*

  In order to motivate a young or middle-aged adult, the diabetes educator focuses on something that is developmentally characteristic for these age groups. For example, a return to work may be a motivator for these patients.

- Later Years Adults

  Older adults typically benefit from short, simple explanation as well as clarification and reclarification until they comprehend the material.

Some examples of communication techniques that are most effective for each age group are as follows:

- *Infant* - soothing touch, being held and lullabies

- *Toddler* - simple concrete terms and short discussions

- *Pre-School Child* - simple explanations and moderately brief discussions

- *School Age Child* – the encouragement of questions and more detailed explanations, as based on the child's level of understanding and cognition

- *Adolescents and Adults* - encourage questions and communicate at a level that is understandable to the receiver of the message

- *Older Adults* - short and simple explanations at the level that is understandable to the patient

INSTRUCTIONAL METHODS

The teaching strategies, also known as teaching methodologies, have to be consistent with the identified learning need, the learning objectives, the learning styles(s), the domain and the level of the domain that you want to address.

Each learning need should be addressed with a separate learning objective and a correlate teaching methodology when the diabetes educator and/or multidisciplinary team have assessed multiple learning needs.

Objectives, domains, levels, and teaching strategies can be found below:

ASSESSED NEED	DOMAIN
Blood Glucose Monitoring Machine	Psychomotor
Pain Interventions	Cognitive
Acceptance of Other's Wishes	Affective
	DOMAIN LEVEL
Blood Glucose Monitoring Machine	Mechanism (Psychomotor)
Pain Interventions	Comprehension (Cognitive)
Acceptance of Others' Wishes	Valuing (Affective)
	LEARNING OBJECTIVE
Blood Glucose Monitoring Machine	The learner will use the blood glucose monitor according to the manufacturer's instructions.
Pain Interventions	The learner will be able to relate how non-pharmacological interventions effectively reduce pain.
Acceptance of Other's Wishes	The family member will internalize a belief in the self-determination rights of others.
	TEACHING STRATEGY
Blood Glucose Monitoring Machine	Demonstration and Return Demonstration
Pain Interventions	Discussion, Reading Material or Video
Acceptance of Others' Wishes	Role Playing

Teaching Strategies Appropriate for Each Domain

- *The Cognitive Domain*

    o Online learning and computer-assisted instruction

    o Workshops

    o Peer group learning

    o Lecture and discussion

    o Independent study

    o Video tapes

    o Audio tapes

    o Reading materials

    o Games

    o Posters and pictures

- *The Psychomotor Domain*

    o Live or video demonstration

    o Step-by-step pictures

    o Simulations and use of medic models

- *The Affective Domain*

    o Props to foster value, belief or attitude changes (such as a day wearing an eye mask to promote empathy for the visually impaired)

    o Role-playing

The Length or Duration of the Teaching Session

Even the most experienced educators can have some problems accurately planning the duration of a teaching session. There are a number of factors that can affect the amount of time needed to effectively facilitate learning. There are some general principles, however, that should be considered when planning for teaching/learning interaction. They are as follows:

- A psychomotor need is best met with short teaching sessions for each step of the procedure or process. This principle is applied to diabetes teaching relating to things like blood glucose monitoring, insulin injections, foot care and dressing changes for a wound.

  The diabetes educator should allow the patient ample time in between sessions so the patient can practice without the stress of another's presence, particularly when the learner is affected with a physical or functional impairment.

- Short-term memory decreases as a function of the natural aging process. Repetition and hence, more time, may be necessary for the aging patient and/or family member(s).

- Children, the cognitively impaired and those with a serious illness and/or pain have a short attention span. Teaching/learning sessions for these patients and family members should be brief and modified, as based on the individual's need.

- Learning is often best accomplished with short sessions over time, when time permits. For example, a cognitive need, such as the need to learn about discharge instructions, is best accomplished with a brief session about the medications the patient will take when discharged and then another session, on the following day, that teaches the patient about the community resources that could be of benefit to the patient.

- Heterogeneous (mixed groups of varying knowledge) and large groups tend to require more time for a teaching session than homogeneous (similar group members in terms of knowledge) or smaller groups.

TEACHING AND COUNSELING

The ADA Guidelines: The Classifications of Diabetes

There are several types or classifications of diabetes including prediabetes, type 1 diabetes, type 2 diabetes, gestational diabetes and diabetes from miscellaneous causes.

- *Prediabetes*

  Most people who are diagnosed with prediabetes have had a history of prediabetes regardless of whether they have been diagnosed. Prediabetes is a higher than normal blood glucose level that has not yet reached the diagnostic criteria for the diagnosis of type 2 diabetes. Prediabetes is sometimes referred to as impaired glucose tolerance.

  The affected individual is usually asymptomatic and only learns that they are prediabetic when they are being tested, or screened, for diabetes.

  The Treatment

  The aim of treatment for prediabetes is to prevent the development of type 2 diabetes with a combination of diet, weight reduction, and exercise. If successful, the patient's blood glucose levels should return to normal.

- *Type 1 Diabetes Mellitus*

  Type 1 diabetes, formerly known as juvenile diabetes, is caused by the lack of insulin. The pancreas does not produce insulin because of some pancreatic β-cell damage that is autoimmune, and sometimes idiopathic, in nature.

  This form of diabetes typically develops during childhood or adolescence, however, it can also appear as late as during adulthood with latent β-cell destruction.

  The Risk Factors

  Some of the risk factors associated with type 1 diabetes include:

  - Ethnic groups such as Sardinians and Scandinavians (genetic risk)

  - Cellular abnormalities such as the presence of autoantigens and other proteins in the β-cells

  - Viruses such as rubella, Epstein-Barr and retroviruses that lead to an immune response

117

- o Diet, such as cow's milk for infants, nitrates in water and low vitamin D have been linked to type 1 diabetes

- o A family history of type 1 diabetes mellitus

- *Type 2 Diabetes Mellitus*

Type 2 diabetes, formerly known as adult onset diabetes, results from an insufficient amount of insulin to meet the body's needs. Insulin secretion is insufficient because the affected patient has become resistant to insulin. The combination of impaired peripheral glucose uptake and excessive hepatic glucose production lead to the hyperglycemia that is characteristic of type 2 diabetes. This type of diabetes is the most common classification of diabetes.

The Risk Factors

Some of the risk factors associated with type 2 diabetes are:

- o *Age*. People over the age of 65 years of age have impaired glucose tolerance as the result of some normal changes associated with the aging process, such as increased body fat and decreased muscle mass. This age group is at greatest risk. Those over 45 years of age are also at risk before the normal changes of aging occur.

- o *Childhood obesity*. More and more children are developing type 2 diabetes as the result of obesity.

- o *Ethnicity*. Asians, Hispanics, black Americans and Native American Indians are at greater risk than other ethnic groups (genetic factors).

- o *Lifestyle*. A sedentary life style without regular exercise places a person at risk for type 2 diabetes.

- o *Family history*. A family history of diabetes (genetics) also places a person at risk for type 2 diabetes.

- o *Previous medical history*. A history of impaired glucose regulation, hypertension, polycystic ovary syndrome, high triglycerides, which increase insulin resistance, dyslipidemia, which is a condition in which the patient has abnormal concentrations of lipids and lipid protein levels in their blood, gestational diabetes, or the delivery of a baby > 4.1 kg places a person at risk for this chronic disorder.

o *Bodyweight.* Obesity, particularly with the lack of exercise and other poor lifestyle choices such as alcohol use/abuse are risk factors, is a risk for type 2 diabetes.

o *Low birth weight.* A low weight at birth has been positively correlated with insulin resistance in later life. This may possibly be related to some prenatal impacts on the fetus' glucose metabolism.

- *Gestational Diabetes*

Although women with previously diagnosed type 1 and type 2 diabetes may experience challenges in terms of control during pregnancy, some women develop gestational diabetes during pregnancy without any previous history of this endocrine disorder.

Gestational diabetes typically appears about the 24th week of gestation. Although many pregnant women with gestational diabetes are at risk for future type 2 diabetes, some do not progress to type 2 diabetes.

The Risk Factors

Some of the risk factors associated with gestational diabetes include insulin resistance, obesity, and insulin deficiency. It is also more commonly associated with Native Americans, Pacific Islanders, Mexican and Asian populations.

The Complications

Gestational diabetes poses both maternal and fetal risks in terms of mortality and morbidity. Some of the complications of gestational diabetes that affect the developing fetus include hyperviscosity, respiratory distress, hypocalcaemia, hypoglycemia, hyperbilirubinemia, polycythemia, and fetal macrosomia, which is a birth weight of more than 4500 g. Some of the maternal complications associated with gestational diabetes include spontaneous abortion and preeclampsia.

The Diagnosis of Gestational Diabetes

The testing done for the diagnosis of gestational diabetes includes:

- An oral glucose tolerance test
- Random plasma glucose of > 200 mg/dL
- Fasting plasma glucose of >126 mg/dL. The normal fasting glucose in pregnancy is about 75 mg/dL.

Preventative screening is done in two steps. Initially a 50 g oral glucose load is given and the glucose level is taken in one hour. If the glucose level is more than 130 mg/dL, it is followed with a 100 g oral glucose load. If the blood glucose level after 3 hours is more than 145 mg/dL, it is suggestive of gestational diabetes.

<u>The Treatment</u>

Gestational diabetes is treated with careful monitoring, strict control and the monitoring for, and the immediate treatment of, any complications.

The American Diabetes Association's dietary guidelines are used to develop an individualized dietary plan for the pregnant woman; this diet consists of three meals and three snacks per day. Control is also achieved with the self-monitoring of blood glucose levels and insulin. The degree of control is checked every trimester with a Hb A1C level.

- *Miscellaneous Types of Diabetes*

Pancreatic origins of diabetes can arise as the result of hemochromatosis, cystic fibrosis and pancreatic disorders such as pancreatitis. Endocrine disorders such as acromegaly and Cushing's syndrome can lead to diabetes; and drug induced diabetes can occur as the result of drugs and minerals such as niacin, protease inhibitors, glucocorticoids, and β-blockers

The Role of Insulin in the Body

Insulin is a hormone needed to convert sugar, starches and other foods into the energy needed for daily life. Insulin makes the cells in the human body absorb glucose from the blood. The glucose is then stored in the liver and the muscles as glycogen. These actions prevent the human body from using fat as an energy source.

The pancreas produces digestive juices, insulin and other digestive hormones. Insulin and other hormones are specifically produced in the endocrine pancreas. The pancreas has Islets of Langerhans that contain the B-cells that synthesize the insulin within them.

Insulin is released when protein is ingested and when blood glucose is present in the blood. Blood glucose levels rise after eating carbohydrates. Glucose is only able to enter the body's cell when insulin is present; the body's cells need glucose in order to function properly.

The Risk Factors Associated With Diabetes

Some of the risk factors associated with diabetes are modifiable and changeable and others are not. For example, obesity, poor dietary consumption habits and the lack of exercise can be eliminated with weight reduction, a healthy diet and an exercise routine, respectively. Other risk factors like genetics, a family history and a past medical history cannot be changed or eliminated.

Diabetes educators focus their education activities on the elimination of modifiable risk factors and the control of the diabetes.

The Signs and Symptoms of Diabetes

The most common symptoms of diabetes mellitus are the direct result of hyperglycemia and they include:

- Hyperglycemia

- Polyuria, or urinary frequency, and polydipsia which is excessive thirst, occur as a result of osmotic diuresis secondary to glycosuria

- Dehydration which can lead to fatigue, changes in mental status and weakness

- Orthostatic hypotension

- Nausea, vomiting, blurring of vision, and unintentional weight loss as the result of the hyperglycemia

Patients with type 1 diabetes typically present with the signs and symptoms of hyperglycemia and often, also, diabetic ketoacidosis. Patients with type 2 diabetes typically present asymptomatic or with the signs of hyperglycemia. Those who are asymptomatic often learn about their diagnosis of diabetes after routine screening or testing.

After diagnosis and treatment, some patients experience a temporary and transient period of time where the blood glucose levels are normal, or nearly normal, after acute onset of the disease because the insulin secretion recovers somewhat. This phenomena is referred to as the "honeymoon phase".

The Diagnosis of Diabetes Mellitus

The diagnoses of diabetes mellitus is made after these three tests.

- Fasting plasma glucose (FPG) levels

- A random glucose value > 200 mg/dL may be diagnostic evidence of diabetes mellitus.

- Glycosylated Hb (HbA$_{1c}$)

   HbA$_{1c}$, which reflects blood glucose levels during the past three months, is now a common test used for the diagnosis of diabetes mellitus. The current diagnostic criteria for the diagnosis of diabetes mellitus is an HbA$_{1c}$ that is greater than, or equal to, 6.5%; risk for diabetes and prediabetes is characterized with an HbA$_{1c}$ of 5.7% to 6.4%.

Although there are times that HbA$_{1c}$ findings may be falsely high or low and there is a lack of reliable bedside, or point of care HbA$_{1c}$ testing, a laboratory HbA$_{1c}$ level is useful for the diagnosis of diabetes. Point of care HbA$_{1c}$ testing is useful for monitoring glycemic control, but not for the diagnosis of diabetes mellitus.

Treatment Options

With Type 1 diabetes, the pancreas stops producing insulin or it produces only a small amount of insulin that is not sufficient to sustain life. The injection of insulin, therefore, is necessary and essential to maintain the blood glucose levels within normal limits.

Patients with Type 2 diabetes may be able to manage their diabetes by altering their diet and exercise routines. Some patient's need more than a change in diet or exercise, and their physicians may prescribe an oral medication and/or insulin to help keep their blood glucose levels within the normal target range. Over time, as the diabetes progresses, a patient who was able to manage with diet and exercise alone may need oral medications and/or insulin to manage their blood glucose levels.

There are six classifications of medications that are used in the United States to manage blood glucose levels. These pharmacological classifications are:

1. Sulfonylureas
2. Meglitinides
3. Biguanides
4. Thiazolidinediones
5. Alpha-glucosidase inhibitors
6. DPP-4 inhibitors

Goals of Treatment

In order to manage a patient's goals of treatment, the diabetes educator and the rest of the healthcare team, in collaboration with the patient must establish a plan of care and goals of treatment. It is then the responsibility of the team to follow up and monitor the patient in an ongoing basis.

The American Diabetes Association offers an ABC approach to diabetes management.

- *A1C* – "The blood check with a memory," the A1C check is able to tell what a patient's blood glucose level has been for a two to three-month period

- *Blood pressure* - A patient's blood pressure numbers reflect the force of the blood inside their blood vessels. When the blood pressure is high, it means that their heart has to work harder than it should.

- *Cholesterol* - A patient's cholesterol numbers reflects the amount of fat they have in their blood. LDL is bad cholesterol, and it can clog the blood vessels and lead to heart disease; whereas HDL is the good cholesterol that protects the heart and its functioning. The risk of heart attack or stroke increase as LDL and triglycerides rises. Patients should be instructed to, and encouraged to, modify their diet to avoid these serious life changing risks.

LIVING WITH DIABETES

Patients and family members affected with diabetes have to learn how to cope with diabetes and be able to live a high quality satisfying life despite the presence of this chronic illness and its associated complications.

Some of the psychosocial adaptations that the diabetes educator can assist the patients with include coping, coping skills, depression, anxiety, fear, loss and grief.

Psychosocial Adaptation: Stress, Coping, Depression, Anxiety, and Loss of Control

Stressors can be biophysical, emotional or psychological, social, spiritual, cultural, and intellectual. Stressors can also be classified as intrinsic, innate or internal, in contrast to extrinsic and external stressors. Stressors have to be coped with or they can lead to many complications, including anxiety, physiological alterations and depression.

According to the adaptation models of health, health is a function of how successfully the patient is able to flexibly cope when they are faced with health related problem. Disease occurs with maladaptation; and health is facilitated with successful coping skills. Coping methods can be healthy and adaptive; other coping strategies are unhealthy and maladaptive.

- *Depression*

  Depression of varying degrees often affects the patient and those close to the patient when the person is affected with a serious illness like diabetes. Depression leads to physical, emotional and cognitive changes.

- *Anxiety*

  Anxiety affects the patient with feelings of dread, discomfort, and apprehension. Anxiety leads to autonomic responses and the anticipation of danger. Anxiety can be relieved with patient education, emotional support and medications when indicated.

- Loss of Control

  Humans strive for control, autonomy, and independence in all aspects of their life. These factors often change when illness and disease occur. These losses, like other losses, can lead to grief and grieving.

  The loss of control and independence can result from physical, psychological and social forces. For example, a patient with diabetes may lose a degree of independence, and they can also lose control over their destiny and their bodily changes. Similarly, a patient may experience psychological depression, which impacts on their life and their quality of life. Still more may lose control in the social arena. They may no longer be able to support the family and they may lose control in terms of their interpersonal relationships and roles, including intimate relationships.

Diabetes educators must assess the patient's psychological feelings relating to the loss of independence and control. All patients should be encouraged to be as independent as possible in terms of decision-making and self-care activities. All physical, psychological and social barriers should be identified and eliminated to the greatest extent possible.

Psychosocial Adaptation Techniques

There are several different measures and techniques, aside from medications, that can be used to relieve some of the psychosocial effects of diabetes. Some of the techniques can be more helpful to one patient, where others may be more helpful to others. There are some patients who even use a combination of measures to achieve the relief they need.

- *Massage*

  Massage decreases stress and pain. Relaxation techniques, soothing music and soft lighting, combined with massage, is a great way to help to alleviate stress and pain to promote sleep, rest and circulation.

  Massage can include hand massage, back massage, foot soaking and massage, and neck massage. A warm lotion or oil is used for massage.

- *Meditation*

  Meditation is proven to reduce fatigue, stress and anxiety, all of which can be experienced by diabetic patients. During meditation, the patient should be instructed to concentrate on one's breathing while repeating positive and calming phrases in one's mind. Meditation is spiritual, whereas prayer is often religious.

- *Prayer*

Prayer is a helpful method for religious diabetic patients and their loved ones. Prayers can be religious in nature, though there are some that are non-religious. They can be composed of specific prayers that are associated with their religion or prayers that are in one's own words.

- *Deep Breathing*

  Deep breathing techniques are shown to be effective with tension, anxiety and fatigue.

- *Progressive Muscular Relaxation*

Progressive muscular relaxation (PMR) therapy aims at reducing the feeling of tension, to lower perceived stress, and to induce relaxation in the patient. It involves progressively tensing and releasing of major skeletal muscle groups. Its goal is to reduce the stimulation of the autonomic and central nervous system and to increase parasympathetic activity.

Patients who use progressive muscular relaxation have reported a reduction in their state of anxiety, pain, and their symptoms of depression. It also improves their sleeping habits as well as their overall quality of life.

- *Distraction*

  Distraction is turning one's attention to something other than the patient's distressing thoughts and pain. Some forms of distraction are watching television, talking on the telephone, or other things that can help the patient take their minds off of the pain they are experiencing.

- *Imagery*

  Imagery, also referred to as guided imagery or visualization, consists of mental exercises designed to allow the mind to influence the health and wellbeing of the body. The patient creates a kind of purposeful daydream by imagining sights, smells, tastes or other pleasant sensations.

  Imagery is helpful in reducing stress, anxiety, and depression, manage pain, and to lower blood pressure. Overall, imagery aims at creating an overall feeling of being in control.

- *Biofeedback*

  Biofeedback is a method of treatment in which the patient is able to use monitoring devices to help consciously control physical processes that are normally controlled automatically by the body. For example, body temperature, heart rate, sweating, blood pressure, and muscle tension can be controlled.

  It has been shown that biofeedback can help patients with pain, sleep difficulties and can help to improve the patient's overall quality of life.

- *Hypnosis*

  Self-hypnosis and hypnosis produces a state that includes relaxation and deep concentration. It is helpful for reducing pain, fear, anxiety and fatigue.

- *Transcutaneous Nerve Stimulation (TENS)*

A transcutaneous nerve stimulator, also referred to as a TENS unit, is used as a method of pain relief, by transmitting low-voltage electrical impulses through electrodes that are placed on the skin on or around painful areas.

This device can provide the patient with a short-term relief of pain, but it has not been shown to provide long-term relief.

- *Acupuncture*

This ancient Chinese medical treatment places very thin needles in the skin, and has been shown to help to reduce pain, nausea and vomiting.

- *Acupressure*

Acupressure is similar to acupuncture, but it uses pressure instead of needles. It can be quite helpful for nausea.

- *Mind-Body Exercises*

Mind-body exercises combine deep focused breathing, movement and meditation. These exercises can help the diabetes patient combat stress, depression and fatigue. Yoga and tai chi are two examples of mind-body exercises.

ROLES AND RESPONSIBILITIES

The Patients' Bill of Rights and Patient Responsibilities

According to the American Hospital Association, all patients have the right to:

- Respect and dignity
- Choose their own doctor(s)
- Privacy
- Confidentiality
- Freedom from abuse and neglect
- Control their finances and personal property
- Know about their medical condition and treatments
- Make decisions about their medical care
- Competent care
- Religious and social freedom
- Accurate bills for services given
- Complain and be heard

The Responsibilities of the Patient

Patients also have responsibilities relating to their behavior and medical care. They are responsible to give complete information relating to their past and present health concerns and conditions, including medications, signs and symptoms. They must communicate safety concerns and any lack of understanding relating to their state of health and treatments, or interventions.

Patients are also responsible for participating actively in all aspects of care and treatment, including discharge planning, and providing health insurance information. Patient behavior responsibilities include following all the facility's policies and procedures, and acting in a manner that is cooperative as well as considerate of the rights of others. The patient is the primary decision maker and the center of care.

The Responsibilities of Family and Significant Others

The family and significant others have a moral responsibility to care fro the patient when the patient needs assistance and these supports have the knowledge, skills and abilities to do so, and the patient chooses to have their assistance.

The Responsibilities of the Healthcare Profession

Healthcare facilities, healthcare service providers and all healthcare professions are responsible and accountable for provide safe, high quality and competent care that is complete, appropriate and timely and specific to the patients' needs without any risks.

Methods to fulfill these healthcare responsibilities in term of quality management and patient safety are discussed below.

Collaboration and Decision Making

Decision-making can be done with deductive reasoning and inductive reasoning. Deductive reasoning is reaching a conclusion based on a premise; inductive reasoning is the ability to draw a generalization from a set of facts.

Good decision-making is greatly enhanced with divergent thinking. Divergent thinking, the opposite of convergent thinking, promotes the generation of multiple, creative solutions, rather than one "right" solution or answer to the problem, issue or concern. It is often referred to as "thinking out of the box". Convergent thinking, on the other hand, is characterized by a group agreeing to and coming to common and less creative solutions.

The steps of decision making include:

- Identifying and defining the problem and the purpose of the decision-making. If this step is not accurately performed, the entire decision making process could lead to failure.

- Establishing criteria relating to the desired decision

- Ranking and weighing the criteria in terms of their importance

- Exploring the possible alternatives according to the established criteria

- Deciding on the best alternative as based on the consideration of the potential benefits versus the potential risks

- Making the decision or course of action

- Implementing the decided upon course of action

- Evaluating the outcome of the course of action in terms of its effectiveness

Collaboration and Problem Solving

The problem solving process, similar to the decision making process, has these steps:

- *Problem Definition*

   The most commonly occurring cause of problem solving failures is a failure to clearly define the problem. It is very important to separate the problem from the symptoms of

133

the problem during this stage and to clearly and accurately define the problem at hand.

- *Data Collection*

Data and information relating to the problem are collected and organized.

- *Data Analysis*

Data is analyzed during this stage and the initial problem definition is further refined as based on this data analysis.

- *Generating Possible Solutions to the Problem*

Open mindedness, creativity and the lack of bias can ensure a wide array of potential solutions.

- *Selecting the Best Possible Solution*

All potential solutions are considered. Next, the best possible solution that has the best chance of success and with the fewest possible risks is selected. The diabetes educator must also consider possible solutions in terms of its feasibility, its cost effectiveness, and other issues, such as legal and ethical concerns.

- *Implementing the Solution or Planned Change*

The diabetes educator must evaluate the effects of this planned change as it is being implemented. Some solutions may lead to unanticipated risks and harm.

- *Evaluating the Result of the Implemented Solution*

Has the change achieved the desired goal? Completely? Partially? Not at all?

Other Methods of Problem Solving

- *Research*

The formal research method systematically and formally explores different phenomena and alternative methods. This problem solving approach is frequently used in nursing and healthcare. In fact, evidence-based practice is based on sound research.

- *The Modified Scientific Method*

The modified scientific method is frequently used in healthcare environments, particularly in terms of quality assurance and performance improvement studies. It is less rigorous and time consuming than the research method described above. It, too, often leads to effective problem solving solutions.

- *Trial and Error*

This method is very limited and even dangerous in most patient care situations. For example, the diabetes educator would not use trial and error in a code situation; however, the diabetes educator may attempt trial and error in modifying some patient approaches and strategies, such as motivating a patient, or significant other, to learn about medications and treatments

- *Intuition*

Intuition has mixed reviews. Some view intuition as not valid; others view it as a valid and effective way to know and to solve problems. Intuition does occur as the result of conscious thought, logic or reasoning. Many refer to intuition as an "A-ha moment" or a "gut feeling." Despite the fact that good solutions may be generated with intuition, it is not something that should be routinely employed, because it is unscientific and therefore unreliable.

Quality Management and Safety

Measuring quality has evolved over the years from quality control, to quality assurance, quality improvement to performance improvement and continuous quality improvement. It has also evolved from structure studies, to process studies, to now outcome-related studies. Successful quality management and performance improvement activities improve the outcomes of care, improve the safety and efficiency of processes, reduce costs and reduce risks and liability.

These activities are mandated by external regulatory bodies, such as the Joint Commission on the Accreditation of Healthcare Organizations (JCAHO), the Centers for Medicare and Medicaid (CMS) and state departments of health. Quality management is an integral part of healthcare's responsibilities. Quality management and improvement activities should focus on areas with the greatest risk, the greatest volume, the highest costs and the most problem prone.

Although models differ somewhat, continuous quality, or performance, improvement activities include: The identification of an opportunity to improve a process, organizing a team to work on the improvement activity (those closely related to the process must be included in the group), and identifying patient expectations and outcomes. They also include gathering data and information, including best practices and research studies, analyzing the data, the close examination of the existing process, designing the process with measurable specifications that can be evaluated, and the elimination of all variance. Lastly, they include implementation of the newly designed process, the evaluation of improvement in terms of the measurable specifications, and documentation of the entire procedure that led to the process change.

Quality Indicators

Quality indicators can be categorized as core measures and outcome measures. Core measures are standardized measures of quality. The Joint Commission on the Accreditation of Healthcare Organizations (JCAHO) has ORYX National Hospital Quality Measures that include disease related measures, such as those related to diabetes, impaired peripheral circulation, heart failure and pneumonia, as well as population measures, such as geriatric care, and organizational measures, like those used in intensive care areas.

Outcome measures are used to examine the outcomes of care. For example, mortality and morbidity rates resulting from diabetes, infection rates among diabetic patients, MRSA rates, patient satisfaction findings, lengths of stay and readmissions may be analyzed as an outcome measure.

Structure, processes and outcomes can be evaluated with data. Data can be quantitative or qualitative. For example, the prevalence or incidence of nosocomial infections among diabetic patients are examples of quantitative data. Patient satisfaction and quality of life are often anecdotal narrative comments. This data is considered qualitative data although these two anecdotal levels can also be quantified using a quantitative measurement scale or tool so they can be analyzed and evaluated with quantitative statistical analysis.

Outcomes will be unpredictable and filled with variances if the process and the structure are not stable. Unstable structures and processes will lead to unstable outcomes. The goal is to achieve and maintain stable and predictable high quality outcomes, so good structures and processes must be in place and concretized before outcomes can be stabilized, improved and optimized.

Organizations and diabetes educators can, and should, measure outcomes relating to physiological or biological health problems, psychological status, quality of life, functional abilities, infections, diabetic patient goal attainment, safety, and the occurrence of adverse events. This measurement can involve the measurement of performance over time in a longitudinal manner to determine if planned changes have sustained increased performance, and to identify problems and opportunities for improvement.

Risk Management

Risk management is closely aligned with continuous quality improvement, but instead of proactively planning change like quality improvement, risk management aims to identify and reduce liability by eliminating risks and liabilities that can include patient related risks, quality risks, and financial risks and liabilities.

Risk management identifies and eliminates hazards relating to basic safety, such as falls, elopement, and infant abduction, a wide variety of medical errors, such as wrong site surgery, wrong patient surgery, and medication errors. It is important to note that using a faulty blood glucose monitor can lead to medical errors as well. JCAHO has requirements relating to medical errors in terms of reporting sentinel events and the elimination of hazards using root cause analysis.

Root Cause Analysis

Root cause analysis is a process used to dig down to the deep reasons why mistakes and errors occur. These reasons are usually procedures and processes and *not* people. Root cause analysis occurs in a blame-free environment with teams of stakeholders who closely analyze faulty processes with a number of techniques such as brainstorming, flow charting, fishbone diagrams, data collection and statistical data analysis.

All sentinel events should be examined using root cause analysis. A sentinel event is an occurrence that leads to, or has the potential to lead to, an adverse outcome. For example, when a patient has a left leg amputation instead of a right leg amputation, it leads to liability and actual harm. On the other hand, when a diabetes educator is about to administer an incorrect dosage of insulin while demonstrating the technique to the patient and they suddenly realize that they are about to err and they stop and correct the dosage, it is also a sentinel event. Even "near misses" are considered sentinel events.

The processes that cause harm as well as those that lead to "near misses" must be refined and improved so that all possible human errors are eliminated and future sentinel events can be prevented.

Some of the most commonly occurring medical error sentinel events include the unintended retention of a foreign body after surgery or another invasive procedure, wrong patient/wrong site/ wrong procedure, treatment delays, suicide, operative and post-operative complications, falls, criminal events, medication errors, perinatal death and other unanticipated events.

Peer Review

Peer review is another strategy that can be used to identify opportunities for improvement. With this type of review, peers, such as diabetic educators, collaboratively work together to critically evaluate aspects of care.

Variance Tracking

There are four types of variance including practitioner variance, system/institutional variance, community variance and patient/family variances. In the context of continuous quality improvement, a variance is a quality defect.

Variances can be random and they can be specific. A random variance is one that occurs, because of things inherent to the process; these variances occur each time the established process is carried out. Specific variances occur because of one specific part of the process. Both of these variances indicate that efforts must be made to correct and eliminate variance.

Benchmarking and Best Practices

Benchmarking and the identification of best practices are superior ways that quality and risk can be objectively determined. Some hospitals provide care that is less costly than others, some hospitals achieve better patient outcomes than others, and some hospitals have lower incidences of sentinel events than others. Diabetes educators should identify these best practices and attempt to replicate these best practices so they can continuously improve the quality of the valuable services that they provide to their patients.

Safety

Falls are one of the biggest and most costly patient-related accidents in health care facilities. All patients should be screened and assessed for falls risk upon admission. If the patient has been identified as at risk for falls, special interventions and preventive measures must be immediately implemented.

Some of the risk factors associated with falls include:

- *Poor vision*

  People who are visually impaired can trip over things they cannot see, particularly in a strange or new environment. Patients should be given their eyeglasses and encouraged to use them.

- *Slow reaction time*

  Older people do not react or respond to dangers as quickly as younger people. For example, an elderly person may fall when they cannot react quickly enough to avoid a puddle on the floor.

- *Incontinence*

  Patients who are incontinent are at greater risk for falls than patients who are not affected with these elimination problems.

- *Confusion*

  People who are confused may lack good judgment and they may not be aware of any hazards.

- *Environmental hazards*

  Patient rooms and areas that have clutter, poor light, high glare, wet floors or an absence of call bells are not safe. The diabetes educator is responsible to keep the patient environment safe and without any hazards.

- *Age*

  Older people fall more than young people. Infants and young children are also at risk for falls. Infants, young children and elderly adults are most at risk for injuries and accidents.

- *Medications*

  Sedation, other medications and medication side effects, such as orthostatic hypotension, place patients at risk for falls.

- *Poor balance, coordination, gait and range of motion (ROM)*

  A person will fall when they can't safely maintain their balance. Many older patients and those that have had a stroke have poor balance and they ambulate with a poor gait, the lack of coordination and diminished muscular range of motion. The assistance of a physical therapist may be highly beneficial to these patients.

- *Past falls*

  Patients and residents who have had a fall in the past are at risk for future falls.

- *Fear of falling*

  Patients and residents will tense and tighten their muscles and be stiff if they have a fear of falling. This fear of falling can lead to a fall and injury.

- *Weak muscles*

  People who have muscular weakness, paralysis and/or neuropathy may fall if help, safety and good patient care are not given to the patient.

- *Some diseases and disorders*

  A patient who has a seizure disorder, arthritis, a stroke or Parkinson's disease is, for example, at risk for falls.

- *Patient footwear*

  Shoes and slippers that are not skid proof are a danger. All patients must have sturdy, skid proof shoes or slippers that fit well.

- *Broken equipment*

  If a cane, walker, wheelchair or wheelchair brake is broken, it can make a person fall. Do *not* use anything that is broken. Report *all* broken equipment and remove it from service immediately.

Preventing falls is a team effort. Special measures and special nursing care must start as soon as any patient or resident is assessed as a falls risk.

Biological Safety: Nosocomial Infections and Prevention

Most nosocomial infections are spread by the hands of health care workers from one patient to another. These infections are limited to only those infections that a patient did not have before they were hospitalized or cared for, but acquired after admission or after care.

The most commonly occurring risk factors for nosocomial infections are prolonged illness and immunosuppression, which can result from an infection like HIV, treatments such as chemotherapy, and some medications. Additionally, all pieces of equipment and nonsterile supplies can harbor and spread nosocomial infections. Nosocomial infections are very costly but eminently preventable.

The urinary tract, the respiratory tract, wounds, and the bloodstream are the most common sites for nosocomial infections. Some of the commonly occurring pathogens include E.coli, candida albicans, staphylococcus aureus, pseudomonas aeruginosa, and enterococcus.

Hand washing is the single most effective way to prevent nosocomial infections in healthcare facilities. Protective precautions, such as standard precautions and transmission-based precautions, are also necessary to prevent the spread of these deadly infections, which is extremely important because of the presence of so many resistant strains of pathogens, like methicillin-resistant staphylococcus aureas (MRSA), vancomycin resistant enterococcus (VRE) and penicillin resistant streptococcus pneumoniae.

Protective precautions include:

- Standard precautions that apply to all blood and bodily fluids and all patients regardless of the person's diagnosis

- Contact precautions to prevent any direct and indirect contact transmissions, as those contained in diarrhea, wounds, and herpes simplex.

- Airborne precautions for the prevention of airborne transmission microbes like TB. These precautions include a HEPA mask and a negative pressure room.

- Droplet precautions are used to prevent the transmission of pathogens that are transmitted with a cough or sneeze. Masks are indicated for these precautions.

Biological Safety: Infections Transmitted By Blood and Other Bodily Fluids

Some of infections and diseases that are transmitted via blood and bodily fluids are:

- HIV
- Hepatitis type B
- Hepatitis type C
- Herpes simplex and other sexually transmitted infections

HIV/AIDS

The etiology of human immunodeficiency virus (HIV) is caused by the HIV-1 and HIV-2 retroviruses that deplete helper T-4 cells. This compromises cellular immunity.

These infections can range from primary asymptomatic infection to overt AIDS, which is often complicated with opportunistic infections that can lead to death. Opportunistic infections can affect the pulmonary system, the nervous system and the musculoskeletal system.

Some opportunistic infections include:

- Kaposi's sarcoma
- Pneumocystis carinii pneumonia
- Candidiasis
- Cytomegalovirus
- Herpes simplex
- Histoplasmosis
- Mycobacterium avium infection
- Salmonella
- Toxoplasma gondii
- Tuberculosis

Other complications include acid-base imbalances, fluid and electrolyte disorders, blindness, and peripheral neuropathy.

Some of the signs and symptoms of HIV/AIDS are fever, malaise, dyspnea, lethargy, skin rash, chills, night sweats, a dry cough, oral lesions, diarrhea, weight loss, abdominal discomfort, headaches, stiff neck, confusion, lymphadenopathy, progressive edema and seizures.

Highly active antiretroviral therapy (HAART) is used for the treatment of HIV/AIDS. The goals of this treatment are to decrease the viral load, to prevent secondary infections, to increase the CD4 T cells, and to maintain the patient in the best possible level of health. Compliance and patient education are critical to the success of this treatment because these medications must be taken for life, they are expensive, and they are associated with troublesome side effects.

Hepatitis Type B and Hepatitis Type C

Viral hepatitis is a major liver infection in the United States and worldwide.

All but the most necessary medications are avoided because the liver metabolizes medications. Chronic hepatitis C is treated with interferon; at times, vitamin K may be needed for prolonged prothrombin times.

Patient-Related Safety in the Community

Driving With Diabetes and Hypoglycemia

The majority of people with diabetes are safely able to drive. There are, however, those who may have some diabetes complications and/or symptoms that can interfere with their ability to safely operate a motor vehicle. The American Diabetes Association (ADA) has published The Standards of Medical Care in Diabetes, which is reviewed periodically to compensate for new information about diabetes. One of the topics included in this publication is the ability of the patient to drive and reasons why some diabetic should not drive. For example, diabetics with retinal neuropathy or peripheral neuropathy should be tested to determine if these complications interfere with their ability to drive.

The ADA warns against "blanket restrictions" on all people with diabetes and their ability to drive and urges that a medical professional decide on driving abilities on a case-by-case basis. The ADA also urges evaluations on certain diabetic patients who have a decreased awareness of the signs and symptoms of hypoglycemia. Hypoglycemia episodes while driving can be deadly to the patient and to others. Diabetes educators should instruct patients about the signs and symptoms of hypoglycemia, the prevention of hypoglycemia, and actions that must be immediately taken when the signs of hypoglycemia occur while driving. For example, the patient should be instructed to immediately pull over and treat hypoglycemia .

Medical Identification

There are medical bracelets, medical IDs, and other medical jewelry that is available to diabetics and anyone else who feels that it is necessary. These medical identifications alert first responders to medical conditions that the person may have.

More sophisticated medical identification systems can include complete, up to date medical information and advanced directives. All of these features help medical personnel to make informed decisions about a patient's treatment and care.

Dental Hygiene

High blood sugar can cause harm to a patient's teeth and gums, as well as their entire body. Type 1 or Type 2 diabetics must manage their blood glucose levels, because the higher their blood sugar level the higher their risk for tooth decay, early gum disease or gingivitis, and advanced gum disease or periodontitis.

Additionally, infections and inflammations that start in the mouth weaken the body's ability to control high blood sugar and high blood sugar is a breeding ground for infection to grow throughout the body.

Dental Caries (Cavities)

There are many types of bacteria in human mouths, and when the starches and sugars from different types of food and beverages mix with these bacteria, plaque forms on the teeth. Plaque's acid levels attack the enamel on the teeth and this leads to dental caries, or cavities. The higher a patient's blood sugar level, the higher the levels of starches and sugars in the mouth and the more acidic the saliva becomes.

Several things lead to cavities:

- The amount of cavity causing bacteria in the saliva
- The amount of sugary and/or acidic foods and drinks that the patient consumes.

Sugar + plaque= cavities
Acid + plaque= cavities

- Poor oral hygiene habits, like inadequate brushing and flossing
- Low fluoride exposure in drinking water and oral hygiene products such as toothpaste and mouthwashes
- Some medical conditions and medications that cause "dry mouth". Saliva is needed to rinse bacteria off teeth.

Signs and Symptoms

Some of the signs and symptoms of dental caries include pain and a tooth sensitivity to sweets and/or cold foods and drinks.

Cavities can be detected:

- Visually: cavities commonly appear as a brown or black spot or it can start as white spot.
- Manually: cavities feel soft and sticky.
- X-rays and new technological advances, such as fluorescent light or lasers, can detect cavities and tooth areas that are demineralized.

When the cavities are small, with just small areas of demineralized enamel, the tooth can be filled, but the conservative approach is to use a prescription-strength fluoride toothpaste or mouth rinse, which is a natural mineral that "remineralizes" and hardens the demineralized tooth.

On the other hand, when a cavity is medium to severe, it is treated by drilling away the soft decay and filling the tooth. Severe cavities are treated with a root canal to save the tooth. The infected nerve is removed. The last alternative is extraction. The entire tooth, including the infected inside area, is removed.

The diabetes educator should instruct patients about ways that they can prevent cavities and other oral problems. Some areas that should be covered in this teaching include:

- *Diet*. The patient should be instructed to limit the amount of sugary and/or acidic foods and drinks that they consume. The patient should read all food and drink labels.

- *Oral hygiene*. The patient should be instructed to brush and floss their teeth at least 2 times a day.

- *Dental sealants*. These sealants are a filling material seeped into the pits/grooves of the permanent molar teeth to prevent decay-causing plaque from getting into the grooves. Sealants are most commonly done in children but adults at risk can also benefit.

- Dry mouth correction. There are over the counter products and Rx products, like Biotene and Therabreath that can help to eliminate dry mouth.

- Regular dental care. Patients should be instructed to get regular dental care, preferably two times per year, so their teeth can be professionally cleaned and cavities can be detected at their earliest stage.

Gingivitis

If the plaque is not removed from the patient's teeth, it will harden under their gum line. This hardened plaque, called tartar or calculus, irritates, inflames and damages the gingival of the gums. It can also lead to swelling and bleeding of the gums. Tartar can only be removed with a professional dental cleaning.

The signs and symptoms of gingivitis include tender and/or bleeding gums, loose teeth, reddened, rather than pink, gums, pus between the gums and teeth, gums that recede and shrink and bad breath.

Dentists diagnose gingivitis with measurements of the gums and x-rays. Dentists perform deep dental cleaning of the teeth to remove the plaque and tartar. Polishing is done after the cleaning to prevent further bacteria from sticking to the teeth. At times, an antibiotic treatment to heal gums, using arrestin, is also performed. Severe cases may require gum surgery to treat the disease.

If gingivitis is left untreated, it can lead to a more serious infection known as advanced gum disease or periodontitis. This destroys the soft tissue and bone that support the teeth, and in time, causes the gums to pull away from their teeth. This can then lead to the patient's teeth becoming loose and falling out. Diabetics tend to suffer from a more severe type of periodontitis because diabetes causes the patient to have a lower ability to resist infections and they are slow healers as well.

Studies rank these gum care elements in terms of the most important and effective to the least effective and important:

- Flossing
- Sonic electric toothbrushes
- Mouth rinses
- Manual toothbrushes
- Waterpik brushes
- Rotary electric toothbrush

Proper Tooth Brushing, Flossing and Rinsing

Toothbrushes

Toothbrushes can be soft, medium and hard. The hard, or firm, toothbrush is sometimes used for serious dental needs, but it has its disadvantages. The hard bristles may take the protective enamel off the teeth and irritate the gums, particularly when brushing is vigorous. Medium toothbrushes may be fine at times for people with a healthy mouth and teeth, but medium bristled brushes have disadvantages. A soft toothbrush is the best choice of all.

A soft toothbrush gently cleans and rids the teeth of soft plaque. It is also good for those that have sensitive teeth, enamel loss, braces and other conditions of the mouth. Hard and medium brushes lead to tooth sensitivity and, since plaque is soft, a soft toothbrush is all that is needed to brush away all the soft plaque. Once the plaque turns hard and into tartar, it can't be brushed away with anything, including a medium or hard bristled brush.

In addition to the characteristics of toothbrushes, there are other choices:

- Manual toothbrushes

- Sonic toothbrushes are the most expensive of all toothbrushes on the market today, but they are good. The bristles move at a very fast rate of speed with a good vibrating motion so that the plaque and staining are easily removed. Some come with an ultraviolet (UV) sanitizer and a timer so the patient will know when they have completed the minimum two minutes tooth brushing session.

- Electric toothbrushes are quite like sonic toothbrushes, but they cost less and have fewer features. The motions of the bristles are consistent with the proper tooth brushing procedure.

- Foam toothbrushes are individually wrapped toothbrushes, which are made of foam, that have toothpaste on them. These foam brushes are good for travel and also for people who are ill and cannot tolerate water and/or more complete mouth care.

Regardless of the patient's choice, the patient should always use an ADA-approved brand name toothbrush.

Toothbrushes make a very good hiding place for germs and germs like wet surfaces. The patient should be advised to always rinse the toothbrush after use and then allow it to air dry in a clean environment. Toothbrushes should be discarded after a month of use.

Tooth Pastes

Some toothpastes have fluoride and flavors; some contain things like baking soda, some are gels and others are paste or powder. Other than choosing a fluoride toothpaste, the patient should also be instructed to only purchase toothpastes that have the ADA approval on the packaging.

Some of the different kinds of toothpaste include:

- *Tartar control toothpastes.* These pastes do NOT remove tartar under the gums but they can control it. To date, only regular dental cleanings will remove tartar under the gums, which is a leading cause of gum disease.

- *Baking soda toothpastes.* Although these products are probably as effective as others are, many people like the squeaky clean feel of these products but the patient should be aware of the fact that some baking soda toothpastes contain peroxide which can lead to gum damage and irritation.

- *Smokers' toothpastes.* These products remove some of the tar and nicotine stains that are caused by cigarette smoking but they are also abrasive. They can cause the gums to recede and a loss of enamel. Smoking cessation is a much better alternative.

- *Sensitive teeth toothpastes.* These toothpastes have a lower abrasion factor than other products. They are helpful to those who have heat or cold tooth sensitivity, which can occur with dental caries, gum disease and/or a tooth root exposure.

- *Tooth whitening toothpastes.* These products have some limited effect on tooth whitening; however, they can also damage teeth.

Proper Tooth Brushing

The diabetic patient should be instructed to, minimally, brush with fluoride toothpaste for at least two minutes at least two to three times a day.

The proper brushing technique is to hold the toothbrush at a 45-degree angle toward the gum line. The goal is to remove cavity and gum disease causing plaque that may be hiding below the gums. All surfaces of the teeth including the front, biting and tongue surfaces of the teeth are brushed. The insides of the cheeks and the entire tongue are also brushed.

Flossing

Flossing between teeth and under the gum line at least once a day with dental floss or an electronic cleaner will remove plaque that tooth brushing cannot reach.

Some find the process of holding and manipulating the floss to be difficult and cumbersome. Pre-loaded floss handles that are sold by the bag are much easier to use and they are just as effective as using traditional floss. Instead of wrapping the floss around the fingers, the person will just simply hold the handle against the tooth to form a "C" around the tooth and then gently move the floss "up and down" in a vertical motion.

Patients who lack the fine motor skills to floss can benefit from a Waterpik® or an air flosser. They are just as good as using regular floss and they are a lot easier.

Flossing must be a regular daily part of daily oral hygiene. The flossing options are also numerous. Any ADA approved floss or device will do the job well, provided it is used properly and at least once a day.

Mouth Washing

The mouth is an excellent place for germs and bacteria to live, grow, multiply and hide. Germs love the mouth. It is moist, it is warm, and it is dark. They find tiny, comfortable hiding places between the teeth, along and under the gum line, on the insides of the cheeks and on the tongue. All of these bacteria lead to plaque.

These germs and bacteria become loosened after tooth brushing and flossing, so the mouth should be vigorously rinsed. The physical force of moving a fluid, like water or mouthwash, will force these germs to loosen even more, and, with the addition of an antiseptic mouthwash, germs can no longer grow and multiply.

Mouth washing should be done after each tooth brushing and flossing session, and more often whenever possible.

Types of Mouthwashes

...loride or whitening agents. Some claim to treat the gums ... people, including diabetic patients, select an alcohol free mouthwash like Listerine Zero® because they dislike the taste of alcohol and/or they are in a recovery program, like Alcoholics Anonymous, and they cannot have any alcohol at all. The same is true for children, pregnant women and nursing mothers. These populations should only use an alcohol-free mouthwash. Also, alcohol dries out tissues, including the tissues in the mouth, so plaque will more easily stick to the teeth with a mouthwash containing alcohol.

The next choice for your patients is to determine whether or not to choose a mouthwash that does or does not include fluoride. ACT® is an example of a mouthwash that contains fluoride. Fluoride fights cavities because it remineralizes the teeth.

Mouthwash is NOT a substitute for tooth brushing and flossing. It is an additional part of oral care.

Here are the steps for using mouthwash correctly:

- Dilute the mouthwash if the label states so.
- Pour out an amount of the mouthwash that will fill about ½ of the mouth.
- Swish the mouthwash around the entire mouth so all surfaces are rinsed.
- Swish vigorously for at least 30 seconds and up to one minute or more.

Skin Care

Every part of the body, including the skin, is affected by diabetes. The majority of these skin problems can be prevented or treated easily if they are caught early enough. Patients with diabetes are at a higher risk for bacterial infections, fungal infections and itching than those without diabetes; and some skin conditions found almost solely among diabetics, including diabetic dermopathy, necrobiosis lipoidica diabeticorum, diabetic blisters, and eruptive xanthomatosis, also affect the patient.

Acanthosis nigricans is a skin condition that appears as tan or brown raised areas on a patient's armpits, sides of their neck and groin area, and occasionally on hands, elbows and knees. Treatment includes weight loss, as this condition most often affect diabetic patients who are overweight.

Diabetic dermopathy is a skin problem caused by diabetes that changes a patient's small blood vessels. This often is seen as light brown, scaly patches on the front of both of the patient's legs, which do not cause any itching or pain. It is harmless and there is no treatment needed.

Necrobiosis lipoidica diabeticorum (NLD) is also caused by changes in the patient's blood vessels, but it is different from diabetic dermopathy in that the spots are fewer, but larger and deeper. Signs and symptoms include dull, raised red areas that can lead to a shiny scar with a violet border and the vessels under the skin may be easier to see than they normally would be. It can sometimes be painful and the spots can crack open. The patient should be advised to contact their physician for treatment if and when these sores break open.

Diabetic blisters are rare but they can occur on the back of fingers, hands, toes, feet, legs or forearms. There is usually no pain associated with these blisters, and the only treatment is to keep blood glucose levels normal.

Eruptive xanthomatosis is another skin condition that often occurs when the blood glucose levels are not controlled. It appears as firm, yellow, pea-like bumps on the skin. Each bump has a red halo and it can be itchy. These blisters will often disappear when diabetes control is restored.

The bacterial infections that most commonly occur among patients with diabetes include infections of the eyelid, boils, folliculitis, or infections of the hair follicles, carbuncles, which are deep infections of the skin and the tissue under the skin, and infections around the nails. The typical and symptoms of these infections include the typical signs and symptoms associated with all infections. They include heat, swelling, redness and pain. Treatments include antibiotics and blood glucose control. These skin disorders can be prevented with good skin care.

Common fungal infections include jock itch, athlete's foot, ringworm, and vaginal infections. The signs and symptoms include itchy rashes and red areas that are surrounded by tiny blisters and scales. Itching can result from yeast infections, dry skin or poor circulation. Treatment includes limiting the amount of time bathing especially when there is low humidity, using mild soaps with moisturizers and applying skin cream after bathing.

Foot Care

There are a number of foot problems associated with diabetes. These disorders most often occur as a result of nerve damage or neuropathy, poor peripheral blood flow and changes in the shape of a patient's feet or toes.

Neuropathy is a common foot problem. It can be painful but it can also lessen a patient's ability to feel pain, heat and cold. This can result in a patient's being unaware of a foot problem until it becomes infected. This nerve damage can also affect the shape of a patient's feet or toes, therefore the patient should be fitted with therapeutic shoes.

Patients with diabetes are also at risk of foot ulcers. These foot ulcers most often occur on the ball of the foot or on the bottom of the big toe, although poorly fitted shoes can result in ulcers on the sides of their feet.

Foot ulcers, even those that do not cause pain, should never be neglected because they can lead to serious infections and limb loss. Patients should avoid walking on a foot ulcer because this can cause the infection to become larger and deeper. If the ulcer does not heal quickly and/or the patient's peripheral circulation is poor, the patient should be referred to a vascular surgeon.

Keeping control of the blood glucose level is essential because high blood glucose levels cause problems with healing and fighting off infections.

Not only does glucose control help the diabetic patient to have better blood flow and improved circulation, the control of blood pressure and cholesterol also helps. Smoking can cause arteries to harden so the patient should refrain from smoking.

Intermittent claudication is pain felt in a patient's legs when they are walking fast, up a hill or on a hard surface. Refraining from smoking, a walking program and medication to help with circulation are treatment options. Exercising and using sturdy and well-fitted shoes are also good for stimulating blood flow.

Social and Financial Issues

- *Employment*

  Financial issues can arise, due to high medical costs that are not covered by insurance and/or the loss of employment as a result of the disease. Many patients and caregivers may be forced to leave their jobs for many reasons including the complications of diabetes and the time necessary to maintain and control the state of health with multiple doctors' appointments and unexpected short-term complications.

  Further compounding the loss of employment income, the patient and/or significant other may often lose their health insurance benefits that were received with their employment status. Although the Family Medical Leave Act offers some buffers, it does NOT insure income during the period of time that a caregiver is not working; it only protects the person' job for a limited period of time.

- *Family and Medical Leave Act*

  The Family and Medical Leave Act, federal law, offers diabetic patient's family members with some minimal, temporary degree of job security when caring for a loved one. Companies with at least fifty employees are mandated to follow the Family and Medical Leave Act. Employees in these companies, who work within seventy-five miles of its location, for at least twelve months, and at least 1,250 hours in those twelve months, can take up to a twelve month leave, without pay, to care for a member of their family.

  Some states are more liberal than others in defining a family member. Federal law considers immediate family members as parents, spouses and children, but some states also allow for others, such as domestic partners, siblings, grandparents and in-laws.

Diabetes educators should advise patients and significant others to consult with the human resources department for the company they are employed by to discuss the Family and Medical Leave Act and how it may help them.

-
- *Insurance*

In addition to all of the other factors that impact patients during illness, financial concerns also affect the patient and the family unit. Healthcare and treatment are expensive. Even with good private health insurance, Medicare and Medicaid, some patients do not have the ability to pay their co pays or for all of the expensive supplies and medications that they need.

Unfortunately not everyone in the United States is covered by insurance for a range of different reasons. There are charities and organizations that can sometimes assist patients with their medical expenses, and most facilities have a case manager or social worker employed that can help patients who have little or no insurance to pay for their medical needs, such as hospital stays, medications, and diagnostic procedures.

- *Disability*

Assistance is provided to people with disabilities, including diabetes and diabetes related complications, with the United States Social Security and Supplemental Security Income Disability programs.

Social Security Disability Insurance pays benefits to patients, and dependents, if they have worked enough during their lifetime and they have paid social security taxes. Supplemental Security Income pays benefits to a patient based on their individual financial needs.

METABOLIC MONITORING

All members of the healthcare team, including diabetes educators, monitor the patients' metabolic status to determine if the patient goals are being met and to determine alternative treatments, including additional patient education, when the patient goals are not met.

Some of the factors that are considered in terms of metabolic monitoring include:

- *Glucose*

  The patient's blood glucose levels are monitored, the testing sites for the glucose testing are inspected, and the meter and the sensor are also evaluated for accuracy.

- *AIC*

  AIC levels are obtained, assessed and monitored every couple of months to determine how well, over time, the patient's metabolic functioning and diabetes are being successfully managed and controlled.

- *Blood pressure*

  The blood pressure is monitored to determine if the patient is hypertensive. Hypotension can occur from a number of factors including stress, uncontrolled diabetes and renal impairment.

- *Weight*

  Weight is monitored in order to determine whether the patient has any significant weight gains or losses. When patients are retaining water and bodily fluids, the diabetes educator should instruct the patient to take and record daily weights

- *Regimen and Record Keeping*

  All patient data is highly useful for monitoring the patient and the success of their treatment plan. As stated above, when data is collected and aggregated over time, patterns and trends can be quite easily analyzed and identified.

V. NUTRITIONAL PRINCIPLES AND GUIDELINES

THE DIABETES DIET

According to the American Diabetes Association (ADA), it is no longer necessary to measure, weigh, count and perform "exchanges" to plan a diabetic meal. Instead, the dinner plate is simply divided into sections in order to guide decision-making relating to the amounts and types of foods that diabetic patients should eat.

The ADA suggests drawing an imaginary line through the center of a patient's plate and then cutting the remaining half to yield two quarters. Now the plate has three sections.

The larger section, the half of the plate, should be filled with non-starchy vegetables like carrots, spinach, lettuce, greens, bok choy, green beans, broccoli, cauliflower, tomatoes, cucumber, beets, okra, mushrooms, peppers and turnips. One of the small sections, a quarter of the plate, should contain starchy foods, such as whole grain bread, high-fiber cereal, oatmeal, grits, rice, pasta, cooked beans and peas like pinto or black-eyed peas, potatoes, corn, lima beans, sweet potatoes, winter squash, pretzels, low fat crackers, or fat-free popcorn. In the last small quarter of the plate, the patient can put protein, such as chicken or turkey without the skin, fish, such as tuna, salmon, cod or catfish, lean cuts of beef or pork, such as the end cuts of a sirloin or pork tenderloin, tofu, eggs or low-fat cottage cheese.

The patient can add an 8 oz. glass of 1% or skim milk, which can be substituted with 6 oz. of light yogurt or a small roll, preferably whole grain. A fresh piece of fruit or ½ cup of fresh fruit salad can complete the meal.

Foods

Increasing the intake amount of vegetables, especially those that are not starchy, and foods made with whole grains should be chosen over those foods that are made with refined grains. Some helpful tips for increasing whole grains versus refined grains are switching from sugary cereals to unsweetened whole grain cereal or oatmeal, replacing regular pasta, crackers and bread with whole grain pastas, crackers and bread.

Fresh, frozen or canned fruit without sugar is always recommended, and healthy fats, such as vegetable oils, mayonnaise, avocado, nuts and seeds, should be chosen, in moderation. Unhealthy fats should be totally eliminated. Low-fat alternative foods and fat-free foods that are not overly processed are also recommended.

Proteins

Patients should also be taught about the importance of consuming proteins. Chicken or turkey without skin and lean beef and pork from the end of the cut is recommended. A great non-meat substitute for protein is eggs and egg substitutes; and vegetarian sources of protein include beans and soy-based products. Fish should be included in the diet at least twice a week.

Beverages

Water is an excellent choice of a beverage for all people, including people with diabetes. Water is the body's natural irrigant. Diabetic patients should also be encouraged to drink skim or 1% milk, unsweetened or artificially sweetened beverages, such as unsweetened tea, diet soda and lemonade sweetened with an artificial sweetener.

Alcohol should be avoided, but if a diabetic patient chooses to drink alcohol the limit is two drinks for men and one drink for women per day.

Illicit Drugs and Caffeine

Blood glucose levels can be affected immediately after taking illicit drugs. Being under the influence of drugs can also impair a patient's awareness of low blood glucose levels and how to correctly treat it.

Caffeine is a stimulant, which can be found in coffee, tea and some types of sodas. Caffeine can causes rises of blood pressure; therefore, patients who have high blood pressure or heart disease should limit or eliminate the amount of caffeine in their diet. There are many decaffeinated beverages that can be substituted for those with caffeine.

Interpreting Food Labels

The diabetes educator is responsible for educating patients about food labels and how to interpret them. The nutritional facts and information on food labels are somewhat confusing but they are extremely helpful for diabetic meal planning. There are several things on these labels that diabetic patients should be knowledgeable about. Some of these things include:

- *Serving size.* It is necessary to know how many servings a can, a box or a frozen food bag contains. Some may contain two, three or four servings. This information is important and it is necessary for determining the serving size and the amount of sodium and other things that are contained in each serving.

- *Amounts per serving.* The amounts of certain things like sodium and carbohydrates, for example, are listed, per serving, on the food's nutritional label. The abbreviation g is for grams, and mg stands for milligrams. Diabetics should be encouraged to choose foods with low calories, saturated fats, trans fat, cholesterol and sodium. They should also be encouraged to choose foods that are high in fiber.

- *Calories.* The amount of calories per serving should be limited for a person who is trying to lose weight.

- *Total carbohydrates.* Carbohydrates include sugars, complex carbohydrate and fiber. Due to the fact that all carbohydrates affect blood sugar, patients should be encouraged to use the total grams of carbohydrates per serving when choosing foods to eat instead of just considering the sugar content.

- *Fiber.* Male diabetes patients should be encouraged to eat 38 grams of fiber a day; and women should consume 25 grams of fiber each day.

- *Sugar alcohol.* Sugar alcohols, also referred to as polyols, include artificial sweeteners like sorbitol and xylitol, and have fewer calories than sugar and starches; however, they are not calorie or carbohydrate free.

- *Total fat, trans fat and cholesterol.* Fats that are good for a patient are mono and polyunsaturated fats; however, saturated and trans fats are not healthy choices, therefore, the diabetes educator should educate the patient to choose foods that are low in terms of trans fats and saturated fats.

- *Sodium.* Blood glucose levels are not directly affected by sodium, but those patients with high blood pressure, renal disease, and heart disease can be adversely affected with sodium. The average intake of sodium, without any dietary restriction, should be less than 2300 mg per day.

- *Other ingredients.* Patients should be encouraged to avoid listed ingredients such as hydrogenated oil and partially hydrogenated oil because they are high in trans-fat.

- *Percent daily value (%).* These relate to a 2000 calorie diet, so any patient who is on a lower calorie diet should be advised to adjust these percentages.

Post Exercise Delayed Onset Hypoglycemia

Insulin sensitivity can remain at a high level for up to forty-eight hours after a patient exercises. This phenomena is referred to as post exercise delayed onset hypoglycemia.

Post exercise delayed onset hypoglycemia is believed to be more common than the hypoglycemia that occurs during and right after exercise. The diabetes educator should inform patients about this phenomena so the complications of hypoglycemia can be avoided.

Post exercise delayed onset hypoglycemia can be prevented with a downward adjustment of the patient's insulin when the patient is planning an increase change in their usual exercise routine.

THE ACUTE COMPLICATIONS OF DIABETES

Some of the acute complications of diabetes include hypoglycemia, hyperglycemia, diabetic ketoacidosis (DKA) and hyperglycemic hyperosmolar nonketotic syndrome (HHNS). All diabetic patients should be fully knowledgeable about the signs, symptoms, prevention and treatment of all of these acute complications of diabetes.

Hypoglycemia

Hypoglycemia, or low blood glucose, is defined as a blood glucose level that is less than 70 mg/dL.

The Signs and Symptoms

Hypoglycemia has a variety of signs and symptoms, which include early and late as well as minor and severe signs and symptoms. Some of the early warning signs and symptoms of diabetic hypoglycemia include dizziness, headache, slurred speech, sweating, anxiety, shakiness, irritability and hunger.

Severe symptoms occur if the early warning signs are not treated. These severe late signs and symptoms include the following:

- Blurry or double vision
- Drowsiness
- Convulsions and seizures
- Unconsciousness
- Difficulty speaking or slurred speech
- Confusion
- Clumsiness or jerky movements
- Muscle weakness
- Agitation
- Coma

Complications

If the symptoms of hypoglycemia are ignored, the patient can lose consciousness. This loss of consciousness occurs because the patient's brain needs glucose in order to function properly. Other complications of untreated hypoglycemia are seizures and death.

Prevention

A diabetic patient must follow the specific diabetes management plan, set forth by their physician, in order to prevent hypoglycemia. They must also monitor their blood glucose levels and make any prescribed changes to the medication dosage when dietary intake is diminished or impaired since hypoglycemia can occur when food intake is poor and/or exercise has increased beyond the normal level.

Treatment

Early recognition of the symptoms of hypoglycemia can generally be treated by oral ingestion of glucose tablets or consuming sugar, which can include eating candy or fruit juice. If the patient is unable to orally ingest sugar an injection of glucagon can be administered or intravenous glucose can be given.

Hyperglycemia

Hyperglycemia, or high blood glucose, is defined as a fasting (8-hour) blood glucose level that is more than 180 mg/dL. Despite the fact that hyperglycemia leads to complications and chronic diabetes disorders, unlike hypoglycemia, it is not life threatening.

The Signs and Symptoms

Hyperglycemia symptoms do not occur until the patient's blood glucose level exceeds 200 mg/dL. It can take several days or even weeks for them to develop at that point, but the longer those levels stay elevated the more several the symptoms become and the greater the risk for the damaging long term complications of hyperglycemia.

The early signs and symptoms include headache, fatigue, blurred vision, excessive thirst and frequent urination. If these early symptoms are left untreated, ketones, or toxic acids, will build up in the patient's blood and urine. This buildup of ketones is referred to as ketoacidosis, which is fully described below.

Complications

If hyperglycemia is left untreated there are several long-term complications that can result. These complications include:

- Kidney, or renal, failure and nephropathy which is kidney damage and impaired renal functioning

- Diabetic retinopathy, which is damage to the blood vessels of the retina, potentially leading to blindness

- Bone and joint problems such as osteoporosis

- Skin problems, including bacterial infections, fungal infections and non-healing wounds

- Chronic infections

- Oral tooth and gum infections

- Cataracts which is clouding of the normally clear lens of the eye

- Cardiovascular disease

- Stroke

- Neuropathy

- Foot disorders including infections, necrosis, and impaired blood flow

If the patient's blood glucose level raises too high for too long of a period, they are at risk for diabetic ketoacidosis or diabetic hyperosmolar syndrome.

Prevention

The prevention of hyperglycemia includes the patient's following their specific diabetes meal plan, monitoring their blood glucose level, and taking any medications prescribed by their physician, which may require adjustments for overeating and the lack of physical activity.

Treatment

A patient can help to keep their blood glucose levels within a normal range by exercising regularly, taking their medications as directed by their physician, maintaining a diabetic meal plan, checking their blood glucose levels regularly and adjusting their insulin doses accordingly to prevent hyperglycemia.

Diabetic Ketoacidosis

Signs and Symptoms

The signs and symptoms of diabetic ketoacidosis usually develop quickly, often within 24 hours. These include:

- Nausea and vomiting
- Abdominal pain
- Weakness or fatigue
- Shortness of breath
- Fruity-scented breath
- Confusion
- Excessive thirst
- Frequent urination

Some symptoms only appear through urine and blood tests, which can be performed at home as well as in a healthcare facility. In the blood, the patient can detect high blood sugar levels or hyperglycemia, and in the urine test, high ketone levels can be detected.

Complications

Diabetic ketoacidosis is treated with fluids, insulin and electrolytes, such as sodium, chloride and potassium. The treatment complications include hypoglycemia, or low blood sugar, hypokalemia or low potassium, and cerebral edema or swelling in the brain.

Low potassium levels can result in the impairment of the patient's heart, nerves and muscles. Cerebral edema can occur when blood sugar level is too rapidly decreased, a complication of ketoacidosis that occurs most commonly among children and newly diagnosed diabetics.

If diabetic ketoacidosis is left untreated, the patient's risks increase and this diabetes complication can lead to unconsciousness and even death.

Prevention

The prevention of diabetic ketoacidosis includes the following:

- Management of diabetes, which includes the patient's commitment to maintaining a healthy diet, exercising regularly and taking their medications as prescribed

- Blood glucose level monitoring, which includes the patient checking their blood glucose level three to four times a day and more if they are under excessive levels of stress or the patient is affected with an illness or infection

- Insulin dose adjustments, as indicated. The diabetes educator must teach the patient how, and when, to adjust their insulin dosage according to their lifestyle, including such things as the level of exercise and the amount of foods consumed

- Ketone level monitoring, which should be performed any time that the patient is under stress and/or ill

- The patient should be instructed to seek emergency care when the blood glucose is excessively high and there is a significant amount of ketones in the urine

Treatment

Patients diagnosed with diabetic ketoacidosis may be treated in the emergency department or they may have to be admitted to the hospital for treatment. Treatment includes a three-step process, which includes the following:

- Rehydration, which includes oral or intravenous fluids to dilute the excess sugar in the patient's urine and to replace fluids that have been lost from excessive urination

- Replacement of electrolytes, which are delivered intravenously to replace the electrolytes lost. This replacement prevents any short term or long term complications that can adversely affect the patient's heart, muscles and nervous system. e cells to function properly

- Insulin therapy, which is delivered intravenously until the patient's blood sugar level falls below 240 mg/dL and is no longer acidic

Once these symptoms are addressed and the patient's body chemistry returns to normal the physician will try to figure out what caused the diabetic ketoacidosis. Additional treatments may then be necessary. For example, if a bacterial infection was the cause antibiotics are necessary. The physician will also determine if there is any risk for a heart attack, and if so, the patient may need a complete cardiac assessment.

Hyperglycemic Hyperosmolar Nonketotic Syndrome (HHNS)

Signs and Symptoms

Initial signs and symptoms of HHNS include:

- Fever
- Convulsions
- Lethargy
- Nausea
- Weight loss
- Coma
- Confusion
- Weakness
- Increased thirst
- Increased urination, which occurs only at the beginning of this syndrome

If left untreated other symptoms can develop over a period of days to weeks, including speech impairments, loss of feeling or function of one's muscles and dysfunctional movement.

Complications

The possible complications related to HHNS are acute respiratory collapse or shock, blood clotting complications, brain swelling or cerebral edema, and increased blood acid levels, which is referred to as lactic acidosis.

Prevention

The prevention of HHNS includes controlling diabetes, recognizing the signs of infection, and the signs of dehydration. The diabetes educator must teach patients about these signs so the patient knows when to act in order to prevent HHNS.

Treatment

The treatment of HHNS includes intravenous fluids with potassium, intravenous insulin and other medications to correct any problems relating to the patient's blood pressure, urinary output, level of hydration and circulation.

THE CHRONIC COMPLICATIONS OF DIABETES

Unmanaged and poorly controlled diabetes can lead to a wide variety of complications, including those that lead to severe disability and even death. A large number of these complications are related to the vascular damage that diabetes causes in terms of both microvascular, or microcirculation, and macrovascular, or macrovascular damage to the small and large vessels of the body, respectively. The control of blood glucose at a HbA1c < 7% can prevent these complications.

Microvascular Damage

Microvascular damage leads to many of the most commonly occurring complications of diabetes, namely, retinopathy, nephropathy and neuropathy.

Microvascular leads to alterations of the integumentary, or skin, system. Some of these complications include poor wound healing, ulcerations, and infections, particularly those affecting the lower extremities, or legs and feet.

- *Retinopathy*

    Sadly, this preventable complication of diabetes is the leading cause of adult blindness the United States.

    Capillary microaneurysms occur in the retina. This is then followed by macular edema. Although the initial stages of diabetic retinopathy is often asymptomatic, it later leads to blurred vision, detachment of the retina or vitreous, and finally a loss of vision which can be partial or complete. The rate of progression varies among individuals.

    Diabetic retinopathy is diagnosed with a retinal examination by an ophthalmologist. This complication of diabetes can be prevented with good control of the disease. The treatment of this complication also includes strict control of the disease to prevent further damage, argon laser photocoagulation or a vitrectomy.

- *Nephropathy*

    Diabetic nephropathy, a renal glomerular disorder, is a preventable complication of diabetes that is the leading cause of chronic renal failure in the United States.

    The pathological changes that occur as the result of diabetic nephropathy include the sclerosis of the glomeruli, a thickening of the glomerular membrane, and mesangial expansion. These pathophysiological changes lead to decreased glomerular filtration rates and glomerular hypertension.

This disorder may remain asymptomatic until the patient develops renal failure or nephritic syndrome. This diagnosis of this disorder is based on the presence of urinary albumin. A ratio > 30 mg/g or an albumin excretion 30 to 300 mg/24 h suggests the early stage of diabetic nephropathy. Advanced diabetic nephropathy is signaled with a positive urine dipstick for protein. This positive dipstick indicates that the albumin excretion is more than 300 mg/day.

Treatment aims to control the patient's blood pressure and the patient's control of their blood glucose. An ACE inhibitor, an angiotensin II receptor blocker, or a combination of both may be indicated to control the patient's hypertension.

- *Neuropathy*

This complication of diabetes consists of nerve ischemia, or death, as the result of a combination of metabolic changes within the cells that alter nerve fiber functioning, direct effects of high glucose levels on nerve neurons and ischemia in the microvascular circulation.

There are multiple types of diabetic neuropathy including the following:

- *Symmetric Polyneuropathy*

    This form of neuropathy is the most commonly occurring form of diabetic neuropathy. It is often referred to as the "stocking glove" type of neuropathy because it affects the hands and the feet.

    The signs and symptoms include paresthesia, which is a feeling of tingling or pricking resulting from pressure or damage to a patient's peripheral nerves, dysesthesias, which is a painful or uncomfortable sense of touch, and sensory losses to touch, temperature, and vibration.

    These sensory deficits can lead to foot ulcerations, infections, which are difficult to treat because of the diabetes, fractures, subluxation, which is a partial or complete dislocation of a bone at the joint, and the destruction of the normal foot anatomy, which is referred to as Charcot joint.

    Small fiber neuropathy is marked with the preservation of vibration and positional sensations and the presence of pain, numbness, and the loss of temperature sensation; and large fiber neuropathy, on the other hand, is characterized by muscle weakness, loss of vibration and position senses, and the lack of deep tendon reflexes. Foot drop is common.

- Autonomic Neuropathy

    Autonomic neuropathy can affect all aspects of the autonomic nervous system. Some of these complications include nausea and vomiting as the result of gastropareses, orthostatic hypotension, tachycardia, constipation, diarrhea and dumping syndrome, urinary and fecal incontinence, diminished vaginal lubrication, erectile dysfunction and urinary retentions.

- Symmetric Polyneuropathy

    Symmetric polyneuropathy decreases ankle reflexes and sensory functioning. It is diagnosed with electromyography and nerve conduction studies. The treatment of symmetric polyneuropathy includes pain management (topical capsaicin cream), the control of the blood glucose, and medications such as tricyclic antidepressants like imipramine and anticonvulsants like Neurontin (gabapentin), as indicated by the severity of this disorder.

- Radiculopathy

    Radiculopathies lead to pain, weakness and atrophy of the lower extremities. Radiculopathies are classified according to the location of origin. Diabetic amyotrophy occurs when L2 through L4 (spinal lumbar nerve roots) are affected; and thoracic polyradiculopathy occurs when T4 to T12 (spinal thoracic) nerve roots are affected. Thoracic polyradiculopathy leads to abdominal pain.

- Cranial Neuropathy

    Cranial neuropathies can adversely affect the 3rd cranial nerve (the oculomotor nerve), the 4th cranial nerve (the trochlear nerve), and the 6th cranial nerve (the abducens nerve).

    The 3rd cranial nerve, or oculomotor nerve, is primarily a motor nerve that controls eye movements. The 4th cranial nerve, or trochlear nerve, which is a motor nerve, rotates and moves the eyeballs; and the 6th cranial nerve, or abducens nerve, abducts the eye.

    When the neuropathy affects the 3rd cranial nerve, known as the oculomotor nerve, these neuropathies can lead to diplopia, or double vision, ptosis, or drooping of the upper eyelid, and anisocoria, which is unequal pupil size. Motor dysfunction occurs when the cranial neuropathy affects the 4th and/or the 6th cranial nerve(s).

- *Atherosclerosis*

  Large vessel, macrovascular, atherosclerosis is characterized with the possibility of myocardial infarction (MI), angina pectoris, peripheral artery disease, strokes (cerebrovascular accidents) and transient ischemic attacks (TIA).

  Again, the treatment includes the control of the diabetes, as well as the control of lipids, blood pressure, using an ACE inhibitor antihypertensive medication, and the administration of daily aspirin as well as smoking cessation, if indicated.

- Cardiomyopathy

  Diabetic cardiomyopathy can occur as the result of hypertension, left ventricular hypertrophy, microvascular impairments, obesity, metabolic disturbances and atherosclerosis, among other causes. Diabetic patients with cardiomyopathy are at greater risk than others for heart failure, myocardial infarction (MI) and heart failure after a myocardial infarction.

- Infections

  Infections of all types are an ongoing threat to the patient with diabetes mellitus. The hyperglycemia of diabetes impairs the normal functioning of the T cells and granulocytes that normally protect the body from infections. Fungal infections, such as vaginal and oral candidiasis (thrush), and bacterial infections of the foot are common. Lower extremity impairments as the result of diabetic neuropathy, immunosuppression, and circulatory impairments compound the risk of foot and leg infections.

  Diabetic foot complications can lead to the loss of a limb when ulcerations, infections and gangrene occur.

  All diabetes educators and all members of the healthcare team must strictly adhere to all standard precautions and hand washing techniques. Hand washing is the single most effective way to prevent nosocomial infections in healthcare facilities. There are protective measures that must be used for the protection of the patients, visitors and all members of the healthcare staff. These measures are discussed in the Biological Safety section, and they are an essential tool in infection protection and control.

- Mononeuropathy

  Mononeuropathies, another complication of diabetes, can cause foot drop when it affects the perineal nerve, as well as finger numbness, weakness and carpal tunnel syndrome, among other nerve compression disorders, when it affects the medial nerve.

- Other Complications

  Some of the other complications associated with diabetes mellitus are rheumatoid disorders, ophthalmic disorders, hepatobiliary disorders, disorders of the skin and psychological complications. For example, diabetic patients often suffer from skin infections, ulcerations and other skin disorders.

Rheumatoid complications associated with diabetes include:

- Carpal tunnel syndrome, or muscle infarction sclerodactyly, which is a thickening and tightening of the skin to the fingers and hand

- Dupuytren contracture, which is a painless thickening and contracture under the skin of the fingers and hand

- Adhesive capsulitis, or frozen shoulder, which is an inflammation of the shoulder that can cause pain and loss of motion

- In addition to diabetic retinopathy, cataracts, glaucoma, optic neuropathy, and corneal abrasions, are examples of ophthalmic disorders that are commonly associated with diabetes; and some of the hepatobiliary impairments that can occur as the result of diabetes are nonalcoholic fatty liver disease, gallstones, and cirrhosis of the liver.

THE PATHOPHYSIOLOGY OF DIABETES

Type 1 Diabetes

Type 1 diabetes is a condition in which the insulin producing beta cells of the pancreas are attacked and destroyed by the immune system. It has autoimmune origins because there are anti-insulin and anti-islet cell antibodies present in the blood. This pathophysiological autoimmune effect leads to lymphocytic infiltration and the destruction of the pancreas' islets. This type of diabetes will not respond to insulin-stimulating oral drugs; it requires insulin therapy by IV or injection.

It is a rapid onset disease that can occur over a few days to a week in time. Other autoimmune conditions related to Type 1 diabetes are hypothyroidism and vitiligo. Vitiligo is a skin condition characterized by patchy depigmentation of skin on the extremities such as the hands.

MODY

Maturity-onset diabetes of the young, or MODY, results from a single gene mutation that encodes a protein called glucokinase. Glucokinase acts as a glucose sensor in insulin-producing beta cells. Insulin production fails without normal glucokinase insulin, thus causing diabetes to occur.

Type 2 Diabetes

A relative deficiency of insulin, rather than an absolute deficiency, causes Type 2 diabetes. There is a beta cell deficiency and peripheral insulin resistance. These two factors lead to high levels of insulin in the blood but there is no hypoglycemia. The main cause of insulin resistance is obesity.

Over time, in the majority of cases, the patient will be required to take insulin, because the oral drugs no longer stimulate adequate insulin release.

Gestational Diabetes

When a pregnant woman has excessive counter-insulin hormones of pregnancy it causes gestational diabetes. This results in high blood sugar and a state of insulin resistance in the pregnant woman. There may also be defective insulin receptors.

MANAGING CARE

Used needles and other supplies and equipment are biohazards because they have been contaminated with blood or other bodily fluids. Used needles and other biohazardous wastes, can transmit diseases, some of which can be life threatening, like hepatitis and HIV/AIDS.

There are several methods for safe disposal, which include the following:

- *Drop Boxes and Supervised Collection Sites*

  There are red boxes, bins and bags used in all healthcare facilities for the disposal of all biohazardous waste. Needles are placed in hard plastic containers, without recapping. Other biohazardous wastes, other than needles and other sharps, are disposed of in specially marked red bags or bins.

  In the community, the diabetic patient can dispose of used needles in many doctors' offices, hospitals, pharmacies, health departments, and fire stations.

- *Mail-Back Programs*

  Sharps can also be disposed of by mailing them in a special container to a collection center for a fee.

- *Syringe Exchange Programs (SEP)*

  Sharps users can also safely exchange used needles for new needles by contacting the North American Syringe Exchange Network at (253) 272-4857 for no cost. The site is www.nasen.org

- *At-Home Needle Destruction Devices*

  Several manufacturers offer products that allow you to destroy used needles at home. These devices sever, burn, or melt the needle, rendering it safe for disposal. An additional alternative in the home includes putting used sharps into a hard container, like an old plastic milk bottle, and disposing of them in their regular trash. Patients should be instructed to contact their solid waste disposal company for specific information relating to sharps disposal.

The Honeymoon Period

The honeymoon period is a phenomena that occurs among some newly diagnosed type 1 diabetes patients. This phenomena occurs within days or weeks after the type 1 diabetic patient is diagnosed and has begun an insulin regimen. Blood glucose levels prior to the diagnosis may have been over 200 but, after a couple of days or weeks on insulin, the blood glucose levels are within normal range and even low. When the blood glucose levels are too low, the physician may order a lower dose of insulin, during the temporary honeymoon period, in order to prevent hypoglycemia.

Many patients who experience the honeymoon period may believe that they are "cured" of the diabetes. Sadly, this is not the case. The islet cells of the pancreas may temporarily begin to resume near normal insulin production because they have been given somewhat of a rest due to the insulin injections. The patient should be knowledgeable about the honeymoon phenomena and the fact that they are not "cured" of the diabetes.

The Dawn Phenomenon

All humans, with or without diabetes, have the dawn phenomenon because of their innate, internal 24-hour body clock rhythms, which are referred to as circadian rhythms. Circadian rhythms produce increased hormone levels of some hormones like glucagon in the early dawn hours, typically from 4 to 5 am.

Because patients with diabetes do not have normal, balancing insulin production during these dawn spikes of glucagon, the patient's fasting blood glucose may be higher than normal and above the expected level.

Patients should be educated about the need to do some mild exercise after a dinner and to have their dinner earlier in the day to prevent the dawn phenomenon.

The Somogyi Effect

The Somogyi effect can occur when the patient takes long-acting insulin, the blood glucose levels drop in early morning hours, and then the blood glucose levels spike as a protective mechanism to prevent hypoglycemia. As a result of this effect, the patient's blood glucose levels are high and higher than expected in the morning.

The patients should be advised to eat a bedtime snack to prevent this blood glucose dip and the compensatory spike of blood glucose levels that are higher than normal in the morning. They should also monitor and record their blood glucose level early in the morning at about 2 or 3 am for several days in order to allow the patient's healthcare team to determine if the patient is affected with the dawn phenomena or the Somogyi effect which are quite similar.

When the patient's blood glucose level early in the morning (at about 2 or 3 am) is low, the Somogyi effect is suspected; when the patient's blood glucose level early in the morning is within normal limits or high, the dawn phenomena is suspected.

Hypoglycemia Unawareness

Because hypoglycemia can be life threatening, the patient, family members, caregivers and even friends and other social contacts should be knowledgeable about its signs and symptoms.

These signs and symptoms include dizziness, headache, slurred speech, muscular weakness, sweating, anxiety, shakiness, irritability, hunger, blurry/double vision, drowsiness, convulsions, seizures, the state of unconsciousness, confusion, clumsiness or jerky movements, agitation and coma.

Sick Days

Illness and fever cause the blood glucose to rise, often extremely high, because the stressors of illness release protective hormones lead to spikes in blood glucose and they also lower the effects of any insulin that is taken. It can lead to ketoacidosis and coma if left untreated so the diabetic patient must be knowledgeable about how to manage their diabetes on sick days.

Ketoacidosis typically occurs among type 1 diabetic patients with illness; and older patients and those with type 2 diabetes are most often adversely affected with hyperosmolar hyperglycemic nonkinetic coma. All of these complications are life threatening without treatment.

The patient should have a preplanned sick day management plan upon diagnosis, which includes:

- The frequency of measuring blood glucose levels and ketones
- Foods and fluids that should be consumed during illness
- Medications that should be taken and those that should not be taken
- Emergency contact phone numbers, including those of the doctor and diabetes educator

The patient should be instructed to notify their healthcare provider when diarrhea or vomiting persists for more than 6 hours, when ketones are present in the urine, and when blood glucose levels are greater than 240 despite the fact that the patient has taken extra insulin as per the sick day plan, according to the American Diabetes Association.

Type 1 diabetes patients should check their blood glucose levels and urine ketones every four hours. Type 2 diabetes patients should check their blood glucose levels at least four times a day and measure their urine ketones when the blood glucose level is more than 300 during the duration of the illness.

The patient should be encouraged to eat and drink according to their own normal meal plan; they should also be advised to drink ample fluids, which is often difficult during illness and with the presence of vomiting. Ample fluids prevent dehydration and they rid the body of glucose and ketones.

Surgery and Special Procedures

Prior to surgery, invasive procedures, and noninvasive procedures the patient may be required to change their routine diet and medications. For example, a diabetic patient who is scheduled for surgery will not have anything to eat or drink (NPO) after midnight the day before; a diabetic patient scheduled for an invasive procedure, like a colonoscopy, may also be NPO after; and a patient who is having an MRI, a noninvasive diagnostic procedure, may be NPO as well for a couple of hours before these procedures.

Diabetic patients who cannot eat or drink prior to these surgical and diagnostic procedures will have levels of blood glucose that reflect the lack of food intake (low blood glucose) when a medication, such as insulin is taken despite the fact that the person cannot eat.

All diabetes patients should ask their healthcare provider, like the gastroenterologist who performs the colonoscopy, the surgeon who will be performing their surgery and the radiologist who will be doing the MRI, etc. about whether or not they can eat, drink and/or take their medications in anticipation of any surgical or special procedures.

Travel

Diabetic patients who travel must be aware of the fact they must bring an ample supply of medications and supplies, and also that they should carry them aboard a plane, train or cruise ship because checked baggage can be lost or delayed.

Geriatric Populations

The geriatric, or elderly, population is affected by the normal physical, psychological and social changes associated with the aging process, in addition to the diabetes.

In addition to some possible cognitive declines, as discussed previously, that mandate modifications of the teaching plan, the patient may also have physiological changes that impact on their medications. For example, the elderly patient does not require as many calories as they did when they were younger; the elderly patient does not metabolize, distribute and excrete medications in the same effective manner that they did in the past; and the elderly diabetic patient may be physically able to manipulate diabetes supplies and equipment like they were able to in the past.

Diabetic educators should closely monitor the elderly diabetes patient's diet and responses to their medications, as these patients often need lower doses of medication than their younger counterparts.

Additionally, the diabetes educator must monitor the patient's sensory functioning , fine motor coordination and strength and gross motor coordination and strength and determine if the patient can benefit from any assistive devices to make up for any deficits. Some of these assistive devices are discussed below.

PreConception Planning, Pregnancy, and Gestational Diabetes

Diabetes educators should educate women with preexisting diabetes about the impact of pregnancy on diabetes prior to conception, during pregnancy and after delivery. Some of the components of preconception education should include:

- Avoiding unplanned pregnancies

- The impact of diabetes on the pregnant woman and the developing fetus

- The impact of pregnancy on the control of diabetes and the disease process itself

- The fact that good blood glucose control prior to the pregnancy and during the pregnancy can avoid complications to the mother and unborn fetus

- The relationship of "morning sickness" nausea and vomiting on the control of the blood glucose levels

- The need for folic acid supplementation of 5 mg per day until at least 12 weeks of gestation to avoid fetal birth defects

- The importance of having a preconception, baseline ophthalmology examination for diabetic retinopathy as well as another during the course of the pregnancy

- The importance of having a preconception, baseline neurological examination for diabetic neuropathy as well as another during the course of the pregnancy

- The necessity of maintaining HbA1c concentration below 6.1% to avoid congenital birth defects; if the diabetic patient has a HbA1c over 10%, the diabetic educator should advise the woman to avoid pregnancy until the HbA1c is within normal limits.

Women who are pregnant should be instructed of the importance of maintain their fasting blood glucose between 3.5 mmol/l and 5.9 mmol/l and they should also maintain their one-hour postprandial blood glucose at less than 7.8 mmol/l.

Additional education for the pregnant woman should also include the risks associated with hypoglycemia particularly during the first trimester, or the first three months, of pregnancy, and diabetic ketoacidosis.

Comorbidities: Hypertension, Depression, Thyroid Disease, Gastrointestinal Malabsorption and Obesity

Comorbidities include hypertension, depression, thyroid disease, celiac, and obesity.

...diabetes are also affected with hypertension. Diabetes educators should monitor the patient's blood pressures and educate them about measures, including stress management and lowering cholesterol that can assist them to manage their hypertension and to prevent complications, such as renal damage, heart disease and stroke.

- *Depression*

Depression, the signs and symptoms and the treatment of diabetes was fully discussed earlier in the text.

- *Thyroid Disease*

Thyroid disease, like other comorbidities, complicate the control of diabetes.

- *Malabsorption*

Malabsorption is a gastrointestinal disorder characterized by the lack of ability to absorb one or more nutrients. It can occur from primary causes like celiac disease and lactose intolerance, and from secondary causes, such as inflammatory bowel disease, disorders of the pancreas and as the result of gastric bypass surgery.

These disorders can impair the absorption of proteins, carbohydrates or fats. An impaired absorption of carbohydrates can affect the control of blood glucose levels. The diabetic patient with an impaired absorption of carbohydrates may experience abdominal cramping and bloating.

All malabsoption disorders can lead to alterations of the normal fluid and electrolyte balances in the body and malnutrition. Diabetic patients should, therefore, be instructed to seek medical treatment and ongoing follow up if they are affected with a malabsorption disorder.

- *Obesity*

Not only is obesity a risk factor for diabetes, it also complicates the management of diabetes and the prevention of complications, as fully discussed above.

Changes in Usual Schedules

Some of the special situations that the patient will need to be educated about include shift work, religious practices and cultural customs.

For example, people like nurses who have diabetes will have to adjust their meal and medication routines along with correlating changes in their sleep and wakefulness patterns. For example, a nurse who works from 7 pm to 7 am will typically sleep 8 to 10 hours during the daytime.

Thus, our example nurse will eat their breakfast at 6 pm before work and have their lunch and dinner at perhaps 11 pm and 5 or 6 am, respectively. Their medications and their blood glucose monitoring will have to also be adjusted accordingly.

Rotating shifts pose more challenges than fixed evening or overnight shifts. The diabetes educator should design an individualized meal and monitoring plan for these patients, as based on their erratic, rotating shifts.

Religious practices, such as days of fasting, pose similar challenges to cultural customs. Again, the diabetes educator should design an individualized meal and monitoring plan to accommodate for these practices and customs.

Assistive and Adaptive Devices

Diabetes educators should, after an assessment, recommend assistive and adaptive devices to accommodate for any impairment that can be lessened or eliminated with these devices. Below are some recommendations.

Visual Assistive Devices

- Portable electronic magnifiers that can be used in the home and taken with the patient in their pocket or purse
- Desktop magnifiers
- Talking blood glucose monitors like Prodigy Voice

The Lighthouse for the Blind is a superior source of good information about assistive devices that can help your diabetic patients.

Sleep Apnea

Obstructive sleep apnea is a disorder in which a patient, while asleep, stops and starts breathing repeatedly. This continues throughout all sleep sessions. The reason for this apnea is the relaxation of the oral and throat muscles, which blocks the patient's airway and causes the cessation of breathing.

Obstructive sleep apnea is the most common type of sleep apnea. It can affect anyone, but in most instances, it affects middle age and older people who are overweight.

The most common symptom of obstructive sleep apnea is snoring, and in most cases the snoring is very loud. Other signs and symptoms include the following:

- Daytime lethargy and narcolepsy
- Intermittent apnea
- Abrupt awakening during sleep with shortness of breath or gasping
- A dry mouth, sore throat, headache and/or chest pain upon wakening
- Hypertension
- Insomnia
- Irritability
- Depression
- Difficulty with concentration

Obstructive sleep apnea is a serious medical condition with a number of complications. Some of these complications threaten the patient's health, whereas other symptoms are a simple annoyance to others, like snoring.

Some of the complications include:

- *Cardiovascular problems:* Hypertension, arrhythmias, hypoxia or hypoxemia, increased risk of heart disease, coronary artery disease, heart attack, heart failure and stroke.

- *Medication and surgical complications:* Medications such as narcotic analgesics and sedatives can lead to increased apnea because they tend to relax the upper airway; surgical patients may experience respiratory problems during and after surgery.

- *Excessive fatigue:* This fatigue can lead to physical, psychological and social impairments. Narcolepsy can be dangerous because the affected patient can fall asleep while driving an automobile, for example.

Patients who experience more mild cases of apnea can benefit from lifestyle changes, such as exercise, weight loss, smoking cessation, the use of nasal decongestants and not sleeping on their backs. Other options for obstructive sleep apnea include:

- Therapies like CPAP for mild to moderate cases

- Medications to decrease daytime drowsiness

- Surgery or other procedures, such as uvulopalatopharyngoplasty (UPPP), jaw surgery (maxillomandibular advancement), a tracheostomy, implants known as the Pillar procedure, nasal surgery to remove polyps, and surgery to remove tonsils and/or adenoids

INTERPRETING RESEARCH AND PUTTING IT INTO PRACTICE

Research

New knowledge is exploding as a result of the proliferation of scientific advances and research. It is very difficult to remain current with this rapidly accelerating body of knowledge; however, it is the responsibility of all diabetes educators to remain current and competent in all these new areas despite the challenges.

Evidence-based Practice

Evidence-based practice (EBP) is an approach to care that encourages clinicians to use the best available evidence, or research, in combination with the individual patient's circumstances and preferences in clinical practice. Simply stated, evidence-based practice is research based practice.

Evidence-based practice begins with research and then this research is applied to the development of evidence-based practice guidelines which are disseminated through a wide variety mechanisms including publications and professional conferences. These evidence-based practice guidelines can and should be applied to practice after the research and the guidelines are critiqued by the diabetes educator.

Some areas of consideration for integrating evidence-based practices into one's role as a diabetes educator include:

- Is the evidence-based practice feasible and practical?
- Do the potential benefits of the evidence-based practice outweigh the possible risks and costs associated with its implementation?
- Is it potentially effective and efficient or is it too time consuming and limited in terms of effectiveness?

Providing an evidence-based approach to diabetes care and education requires that the diabetes educator can:

- Access and appraise evidence (research findings)
- Understand the relationships between research and the strength of evidence
- Determine its applicability in respect to a particular patient's condition, context and wishes.

Critiques relating to the evidence-based practice guidelines include:

- the date of the publication
- the author(s)
- the basis of the guideline in terms of whether or not research was used
- the quality of the comprehensive reference list

- the professional organization that endorses the guideline
- the review of the guidelines by an expert, or expertly, in the field of practice being addressed
- whether or not the guideline has been successfully utilized in practice with optimal outcomes

Some of the databases that diabetes educators use regularly to review research and evidence-based practice are listed below along with the correlate internet link:

- The Cochrane Library
  http://www.thecochranelibrary.com/view/0/AboutTheCochraneLibrary.html

- The Joanna Briggs Institute
  http://www.joannabriggs.edu.au/

- Ovid's Evidence-based Medicine Reviews (EBMR)
  http://www.ovid.com/webapp/wcs/stores/servlet/ProductDisplay?storeId=13051&catalogId=13151&langId=-1&partNumber=Prod-904410

- Medlars
  http://www.nlm.nih.gov/bsd/mmshome.html

- Medline Plus (An International nursing index and IndexMedicus is also included)
  http://www.nlm.nih.gov/medlineplus/

- Pub Med
  http://www.ncbi.nlm.nih.gov/pubmed/

- The Cumulative Index to Nursing and Allied Health Literature (CINAHL)
  http://www.ebscohost.com/cinahl/

- The Directory of Open Access Journals (Free)
  http://www.doaj.org

- The Nursing Center for Lippincott Williams & Wilkins'
  http://nursingcenter.com

VI. PROGRAM DEVELOPMENT AND ADMINISTRATION

THE DIABETES EDUCATION PROGRAM

Certified diabetes educators should be able to design and improve diabetes education programs. Diabetes education programs, unlike individual educational activities, should address all aspects of the overall diabetes education including:

- The philosophy of the program that is based on a theoretical framework, such as Orem's self-care theory and/or Lewin's change theory

- The goals of the program, such as the provision of optimal diabetes education that improves patient outcomes

- The objectives of the program, which should include all phases of the teaching/learning process

- Policies and procedures relating to needs assessments, course design, content outlines, educational activity evaluations, the evaluation of the overall diabetes education program, patterns of communication including patient/family, physician and healthcare team communication and collaboration, committee memberships, patient confidentiality, the marketing of educational activities and confidentiality, among other things. Policies and procedures establish the structure of the overall diabetes education program. Without a firm structure, the processes and the outcomes of the diabetes education program will not succeed. Weak structures lead to weak processes and unpredictable but weak outcomes.

Performing a Needs Assessment

A needs assessment must be conducted prior to the offering of a diabetes educational activity. Needs can be classified as individual or group needs, perceived self-appraised needs or prescribed needs, and data-driven needs.

Individual needs tend to be unique to the individual. Individual educational needs can be assessed by asking the patient what education they think they need (self-perceived need), by observing the patient and identifying learning needs (data driven) and by analyzing the patterns and trends within the data that is included in the patient's record keeping data (blood glucose levels over time) and laboratory data over time, among other data sources.

Group needs can be assessed by administering an educational needs assessment for the group's self-appraised learning needs. For example, the diabetes educator can conduct a focus group of diabetic patients and family members or they can administer a questionnaire that the patients will complete and return to the diabetic educator for analysis.

Below are examples of items that could be included in an educational needs assessment questionnaire.

"I believe that I need, and would like, education that addresses stress management techniques."

1	2	3	4	5
Strongly Disagree	Mildly Disagree	Neither Agree or Disagree	Mildly Agree	Strongly Agree

"I believe that I need, and would like, education that addresses sick day management of diabetes."

1	2	3	4	5
Strongly Disagree	Mildly Disagree	Neither Agree or Disagree	Mildly Agree	Strongly Agree

Questionnaires and focus groups are measures of self-appraised needs. Self-appraised needs have proven to be accurate in terms of patients' actual learning needs.

Data-driven needs are determined with empirical data, such as seeing (observation), hearing (hearing the patient state false statements or misconceptions), touching (feeling sweating on the patient's shoulder which could indicate hypoglycemia as the result of poor glucose control), and smelling, such as can occur when the patient has a fruity breath odor indicative of ketoacidosis.

Data-driven needs can also be identified by aggregating and analyzing individual data and group data. Group data can be obtained from a wide sources including patient satisfaction surveys, quality assurance studies, the incidence of visits to the emergency department, because of a diabetic complication and the frequency of limb amputations among patients who have received education relating to foot care from the diabetes educator.

Individual educational needs should be addressed with individual one-to-one education; and group needs should be addressed with group teaching whenever possible because, not only is a group teaching session more cost effective, it also provides the learners the opportunity to discuss and share their experiences with others who have the same learning needs.

Developing a Curriculum

A curriculum, also known as a lesson plan or course outline, is essential, because it documents elements of the assessment, teaching strategies, learning objectives, included content and method of evaluation. In essence, the curriculum documents and concretizes the process that will address the learning needs; it also serves as an important aspect of outcomes evaluation. For example, if the outcomes of the educational activity do not meet the expectations, as stated in the learning objectives, the entire curriculum should be modified and improved in order to be more successful.

An example of a course curriculum is shown below:

DIABETES EDUCATION

Course Title: Stress Management

Duration: 1 Hour

Date Developed: 1/23/2014

Date Reviewed:

Date Revised:

Target Audience: Diabetic patients and significant others who are not able to cope with the stressors relating to the diabetes and diabetes management.

Planner: (Name of the Diabetes Educator)

Instructor(s): (Name of the Diabetes Educator or Another Person Who Facilitates the Course)

Type of Course: (Check All That Apply)

__X_Live

___ Self-instructional (Internet)

___ Self-instructional (Hard copy)

___ Webinar

Methodology: (Check All That Apply)

__X__ Lecture and discussion

__X__ Demonstration

___ Other : State methodology

Evaluation Method(s): Posttest and return demonstration

Needs Assessment Data Sources: The needs assessment questionnaire and data indicates poor coping.

Purpose of the Course

The purpose of this course is to provide the learner with the knowledge, skills and abilities to use some stress management techniques.

Course Description:

This course contains basic information about stress and how stress impacts on the patient's management and control of their blood glucose levels as well as how to perform deep breathing relaxation techniques.

Learning Objectives:

At the conclusion of this course, the learner will be able to:

1. Define and describe stress
2. Discuss the impact of stress on blood glucose levels
3. Demonstrate deep breathing

OBJECTIVES	CONTENT (TOPICS)	LEARNING RESOURCES
Cognitive		
Define and describe stress	The Definition of Stress The Sources of Stress The Signs of Stress	Power Point Slides:#1-9
Affective		
Discuss the impact of stress on blood glucose levels	The Effect of Stress on the Body • Physical changes • Emotional changes • Cognitive changes • Social changes The Impact of Stress on Blood Glucose Levels • Elevations of blood glucose	Power Point Slides:#10 – 19 Learner Handout on "The Effects of Stress: Manage It Before It Manages You" (See the Attachment)
Psychomotor		
Demonstrate deep breathing		Videotape showing the proper technique for deep breathing Learner return demonstration of the

		proper deep breathing technique
		Post test

Marketing and Promoting Diabetes Education Programs

There are a wide variety of mechanisms that can be used to market and promote diabetes education programs to your patients and other patients in the community. Some of these mechanisms include posters, newspaper announcements, mailings, e mail messages and communication with community, civic, healthcare and religious groups.

With high quality education and effective marketing, your diabetes education can be a significant revenue generator for your organization.

Maintaining Patient Information While Ensuring Patient Confidentiality

Patient information, including contact information and demographic information, should be collected and maintained for informational and data use without jeopardizing the patients' basic rights in terms of privacy and confidentiality according to the regulations associated with HIPAA and ethical codes of conduct.

Any patient information that is collected should be useful. If any data is not useful, do NOT collect it. Some of the patient information that you may want to collect, in addition to contact information so you can maintain a relationship with the patient and significant others, include age, gender, type of diabetes, patient supports, medications taken and date of diagnosis.

The diabetic educator can use this demographic data in a database to analyze it in terms of identifying patients at risk, to identify patients who are in need of education, and to evaluate the effectiveness of educational activities and the overall diabetes education program. For example, levels of satisfaction related to the overall diabetes education program may vary according to age, gender and/or duration of the disease.

Standards of Care

According to the National Certification Board for Diabetes Educators, the standards of care and practice for diabetes educators are, as follows:

CANONS OF ETHICAL CONDUCT

I. PREAMBLE

The practice of diabetes self-management education ("Profession") is a recognized allied health profession. The Certified Diabetes Educator® ("CDE"®) assumes specific responsibilities to physicians or other licensed/registered healthcare professionals, people with diabetes or pre-diabetes and their significant other(s), the public, associates, and to the Profession itself. These responsibilities must be discharged with honor and integrity to assure the maintenance of public confidence in the Profession and to protect the person with diabetes or pre-diabetes and his/her significant other[s]. For the purposes of these Canons of Ethical Conduct ("Canons"), the term "CDE" shall mean any person who has earned the certification offered by the National Certification Board for Diabetes Educators (the "Board"). As used herein, "Committee" refers to the Professional Discipline Committee of the Board.

The Profession exists for the primary purpose of recognizing and advancing the specialty practice of diabetes self-management education (DSME) and support. CDEs are responsible for maintaining and promoting ethical practice, including, without limitation, reporting unethical practices in accordance with these Canons. These Canons, adopted by the Board, shall be binding upon all CDEs and candidates approved to take the CDE certification examination.

C1.2 Ethics, Custom and the Law

Unethical conduct may involve violations of customs and usages of the Profession as well as actions that violate the law and regulations. Failure to conform to these Canons, including conduct that violates moral principles, customs and practices of the Profession, the law or regulations, may be subject to disciplinary action in accordance with the "Rules and Procedures Regarding the Canons of Ethical Conduct" ("Rules"). Disciplinary action depends on the particular circumstances involved and, without limitation, how the conduct in question reflects upon the dignity and integrity of the Profession. The Committee will take appropriate action, if any, consistent with the Rules. Each CDE has a civic and professional obligation to report to the appropriate governmental body any and all evidence that may come to his/her attention involving the alleged criminal conduct of any CDE relating to the practice of DSME.

C1.3 Disclosure of Other Agency Actions

Each CDE must promptly, fully and accurately disclose to the Board any and all investigations, findings, and actions by any government agency, quasi-government agency, licensing board, registration body, or other similar health related agency or body responsible for national, state or local licensing and/or oversight of diabetes education-related licenses, certifications, or the like ("Agencies"). The CDE's disclosure requirement includes investigations by federal, state and/or private payors regarding existing or potential known or unknown billing malfeasance. Each CDE must make such disclosure to the Board within thirty (30) days from the date of the commencement of action by any Agency. Each CDE must promptly and fully cooperate with the Board and with the Agencies.

II. RESPONSIBILITIES TO THE PHYSICIAN AND/OR APPROPRIATELY LICENSED/REGISTERED HEALTHCARE PROVIDER

C2.1 Provision of Services

The CDE shall recognize the person's freedom of choice in selection of diabetes treatment and education and his/her health care provider. Professional affiliations, including employment and referral relationships, may not adversely limit access to services and shall not adversely affect the decision-making process of the CDE. The CDE must adhere to the ethical principles of the Board that shall take preference over business relationships.

C2.2 Scope of Practice

The Certification Examination for Diabetes Educators ("Examination") is sensitive to areas of general practice and contemporary diabetes knowledge across multiple professional disciplines. Passing the Examination verifies core knowledge in the field of diabetes. Holding the CDE credential does not confer any permission to manage diabetes beyond the scope of the individual's professional practice. The boundaries of professional practice are determined by state practice acts. Job descriptions and job functions are determined by employing agencies, not the CDE credential.

C2.3 Services Not Components of DSME

The CDE shall only provide DSME as defined by the National Certification Board for Diabetes Educators. While other services may be provided in the management and treatment of a person with diabetes/pre-diabetes, they may not be promoted or provided as components of DSME.

III. RESPONSIBILITIES TO THE PERSON WITH DIABETES/PRE-DIABETES

C3.1 Evaluation and Recommendation

It is the responsibility of the CDE to recommend diabetes self-management plans specific to the needs of the individual and to provide appropriate educational and learning information to the person with diabetes/pre-diabetes, other healthcare professionals, the public, etc. The CDE shall recognize that each individual person is unique and deserves specific and responsive guidance from the CDE. The CDE shall be guided at all times by concern for the physical, emotional, social and economic welfare of the person.

The needs, goals and life experiences of the person shall be taken into account. All decisions by the CDE must be made with the understanding and intent that the individual person's best interests are the primary concern.

C3.2 Confidential Information

All information related to a person's identity, background, condition, treatment, management plan or education plan or any other information related to the CDE/person or people with diabetes/pre-diabetes is and shall always remain confidential and may not be communicated to any person or entity who is not providing direct medical care to the patient without the prior written consent of the patient or patient's legal guardian.

Information that may be derived from any CDE's peer review process shall be held and always remain confidential by all participants unless written permission to release the information is obtained from the person under the care of the CDE or that person's legal guardian. All information derived in a work place from a working relationship related to the care of a person with diabetes/pre-diabetes shall be held and always remain confidential by all parties. The confidentiality requirements set forth in this Canon C3.2 shall be strictly adhered to by all CDEs unless required otherwise by law or valid court order or subpoena, or if it becomes necessary to disclose such information to protect the welfare of the person with diabetes/pre-diabetes and/or the community. In such an event, any disclosure of confidential information shall be in accordance with applicable legal requirements.

C3.3 Trust and Honesty

The CDE shall be truthful and honest.

C3.4 Fees and Compensation

The CDE shall provide services based on the needs of the individual receiving the services and not solely for personal financial gain. The CDE shall not engage in false, misleading or deceptive actions in relation to the ultimate cost of the services undertaken or furnished. The CDE shall not over utilize or unnecessarily continue services beyond the point of benefit or by providing services more frequently than necessary.

The CDE shall not submit false or misleading information in requesting payment or reimbursement.

C3.5 Practice Arrangements

The CDE shall not: (i) directly or indirectly request, receive or participate in dividing, transferring, assigning or rebating any funds derived from a referral of a patient to any other individual or entity, whether affiliated with the CDE or otherwise; or (ii) profit by means of a credit or other valuable consideration, such as an unearned commission, discount or gratuity for providing services, except for the fees earned for services performed for the patient.

The CDE shall refer all persons with diabetes/pre-diabetes to the most appropriate service provider, taking into consideration the nature and extent of the problem, treatment resources and availability of healthcare benefit coverage, and the likelihood of receiving appropriate and beneficial care. If the CDE is involved in an arrangement with a referring source in which the referring source derives income from the CDE's services, the CDE must disclose all pertinent information to the patient, including without limitation that the referring practitioner derives income from the provision of the services. The CDE shall advise his/her employer of any employer or employee practice which is in contradiction with this Canon C3.5.

C3.6 Compliance with Laws and Regulations

The CDE shall provide DSME and other services in accordance with Federal law and the laws and regulations of the jurisdiction(s) in which they practice.

C3.7 Reporting

The CDE shall report to the Board any conduct that reasonably appears to violate these Canons. This reporting requirement includes, without limitation, self-reporting, and the reporting about other CDEs, in connection with a third party investigation and finding, regardless of whether the investigation has been completed.

C3.8 Delegation of Responsibility

The CDE shall not delegate any task requiring unique skills, knowledge or judgment to an unqualified person. The primary responsibility for services provided by supporting personnel rests with the delegating CDE.

C3.9 Illegal Discrimination

The CDE shall not decline to accept a patient on the basis of race, gender, color, religion or national origin or on any basis that would constitute illegal discrimination under federal law.

C3.10 Sexual Relations with Patient Prohibited

The CDE shall not have consensual or nonconsensual sexual relations with a current or former person under the care of CDE unless a consensual sexual relationship existed between the CDE and the person prior to the provision of any diabetes educational services or the CDE has not provided any diabetes educational services to the person for a one year period preceding the beginning of the sexual relationship or for a one year period after the termination of the sexual relationship. The CDE shall not engage in, require, or demand sexual relations with a person incident to or as a condition of any diabetes educational services.

IV. RESPONSIBILITIES TO COLLEAGUES AND THE PROFESSION

C4.1 Dignity

The CDE has the personal responsibility to conduct him/herself in a manner that will assure the dignity and status of the Profession. Examples of unacceptable behavior include, but are not limited to, falsifying documents, misusing the certification credential, slandering or libeling another, disparaging former employers, disparaging former employees, and misrepresenting one's capacity as a provider of services.

C4.2 Solicitation

The CDE shall not, either directly or indirectly, solicit the patronage of individual patients or students by way of intimidation, threats, harassing conduct, undue influence, coercion, duress, or unwarranted promises of benefits. The CDE shall not solicit a person who is in a mental condition that impairs his/her personal judgment to make decisions concerning the services being offered. The CDE shall not solicit a person in a manner that is inconsistent with his/her obligation to act in a dignified manner as set forth in Canon C4.1 above.

C4.3 Examination

The CDE/ shall maintain the security and prevent the disclosure of credentialing examinations and their content.

V. PATIENT CARE BY OTHER HEALTHCARE PROFESSIONALS

C5.1 Concern about Care by Other Healthcare Professionals

The CDE should exercise appropriate respect for other healthcare professionals. Concerns regarding patient care provided by other such professionals should be addressed directly to those professionals rather than to the patient. In the event that such concerns rise to the possible level of criminal violation, incompetence or malpractice, then the CDE must immediately notify the appropriate credentialing, licensure, or registration authority and, if necessary, the patient or legal guardian.

VI. CREDENTIAL

C6.1 Use of Credential

The CDE shall use the fact that he/she is credentialed only as evidence of meeting the requisite standard of knowledge and competency in the discipline in which the CDE is credentialed, as defined by the Board. The CDE shall not use the credential to promote any services that are outside the scope of practice of a diabetes educator.

C6.2 Endorsement of Products, Medication, Devices or Supplies

While a CDE may recommend the use of specific products, medications, devices or supplies, the CDE credential may not be used to label, suggest or otherwise infer that such products, medications, devices or supplies have been endorsed by the National Certification Board for Diabetes Educators.

C6.3 Employment by Manufacturers, Pharmaceutical Companies or Suppliers

It is permissible to be employed by a manufacturer, pharmaceutical company or supplier as a CDE. However, the CDE credential may not be used in a manner prohibited by Canon C6.2.

VII. APPLICATION OF CANONS

C7.1 Adherence to Canons

These Canons shall apply to all CDEs, including certification examination candidates."[1]

---

[1] National Certification Board for Diabetes Educators (ncbde.org)

Program Outcomes

The overall outcomes of the diabetes educational program should be measured in terms of its structures (policies and procedures), processes and outcomes. For example, the outcomes should measure and determine the effectiveness of the policies and procedures that create the program's structures. Did the committee structure achieve its goals? Was the curriculum design complete and effective? Processes are also evaluated in terms of how effective, timely, complete and effective they are. And, lastly, outcomes, as discussed below, are also measured.

Some other specific outcomes that should be measured include:

- The number of patients who were served on an annual, semiannual and quarterly basis
- The number of caregivers and significant others who were served on an annual, semiannual and quarterly basis
- Levels of patient and significant other satisfaction with the diabetes education program
- The effectiveness of the educational activities and the learning materials in terms of patient outcome

Patient Outcomes

The ultimate goal of diabetes education is to change behavior. In other words, education should improve the patient's control over their disease, as evidenced by changes in behavior and other data such as A1C levels, BMI, bodily weight, quality of life, the number of emergency department visits, the frequency of short and/or long term complications of the diabetes, and absences from the patient's work because of the disease, among other outcome measurements.

Continuous Quality Improvement Activities

Quality assurance and risk management activities, as fully discussed previously, provide very good data with which the outcomes of the diabetes education program can be evaluated in terms of its overall quality and positive outcomes. For example, a quality assurance study that explores the frequency of emergency department visits among patients who have received education from the diabetes educator has rich data with which to measure the effectiveness of the education and the diabetes education program.

Patient Advocacy and Patient Rights

Patient advocacy is a component of practice for the diabetes educator. Diabetes educators act in a manner that provides individual patients and groups of patients with diabetes the necessary educational interventions that they need in order to facilitate optimal outcomes. Diabetes educators have a moral and ethical responsibility to enhance patients' decision making autonomy, the promotion of the patient's well-being, and preventing and resolving any ethical conflicts.

Decision-making can follow the paternalistic, patient sovereignty or shared decision-making models. Paternalism and patient sovereignty do not respect patient autonomy because the clinician makes decisions and the patient makes decisions without guidance, respectively. The shared decision making model upholds patient autonomy because it includes the patient and the diabetes educator in a mutually respectful relationship which enables them to make good decisions with the support of the diabetes educator.

Health Fairs and Community Outreach

Diabetes educators are strongly advised to participate in their community with education programs in any, and all, appropriate settings and venues. For example, the diabetes educator can participate in a health fair screening participants for high glucose or for high cholesterol levels; they can also present a discussion to elderly patients in an assisted living facility or a civic group about diabetes and the signs of diabetes.

All of these outreach efforts serve several purposes including:

- Informing the public about certified diabetes educators, their roles, and the benefits of employing their services
- Educating people who are interested in diabetes and diabetes screening
- Allowing the consuming public to elicit the help and support of a certified diabetes educator

Discrimination

In addition to other laws, all diabetes educators must not, under any circumstances, discriminate against others in the community and at the workplace.

VII. PRACTICE QUESTIONS

1. You are meeting your diabetic patient today for the first time. Which phase of the teaching/learning process will be the first that you will complete?

   A. The health history
   B. Assessment
   C. Introductions
   D. Evaluation

2. Which of the following is a common learning need among diabetic patients?

   A. A knowledge deficit relating to the short term complications of diabetes
   B. Poor technique in terms of drawing up insulin
   C. Misinformation about the pathophysiology of diabetes
   D. The patient is aware of the long term complications of diabetes

3. Which of the following is NOT a part of the planning phase of the teaching/learning process?

   A. Determining teaching strategies
   B. Identifying learning goals
   C. Incorporating learning styles into the learning activity
   D. Determining the patient's strengths and weaknesses

4. You are teaching your patient about the proper use of a blood glucose monitor. What domain of learning are you teaching?

   A. Diabetes education
   B. Cognitive
   C. Affective
   D. Psychomotor

5. Which teaching strategy is most appropriate when teaching a patient about the proper use of a blood glucose monitor?

   A. Discussion
   B. Demonstration
   C. Reading material
   D. Role playing

6. An expected outcome for an educational activity relating to the proper use of a blood glucose monitor is:

   A. The nurse will demonstrate the proper use of a blood glucose monitor
   B. The nurse will discuss the importance of a blood glucose monitor
   C. The patient will demonstrate the proper use of a blood glucose monitor
   D. The patient will discuss the importance of a blood glucose monitor

7. Culture affects which aspects of the teaching/learning process?

   A. Communication and terminology use
   B. Tolerance for low lighting and seating arrangements
   C. The ambient temperature of the room
   D. The choice of teaching strategies for each domain

8. Which is a motivator?

   A. High stress
   B. No stress
   C. Moderate stress
   D. Low stress

9. Which term best describes the diabetic educator's application of research findings into practice?

   A. Benchmarking practice
   B. Evidence-based practice
   C. Professional decision-making
   D. Critical thinking practice

10. You give a 10 item multiple-choice quiz to a group of patients after you teach a class on diabetes and life style choices. What type of evaluation is this?

    A. Formative evaluation
    B. Affective evaluation
    C. Interim evaluation
    D. Summative evaluation

11. Select the teaching model that is correctly paired with its characteristic.

    A. Pedagogy: Learning aims to meet future needs.
    B. Andragogy: Learning aims to meet future needs.
    C. Pedagogy: Adults have little prior experience to enhance the learning of new diabetes information.

D. Andragogy: Adults have little prior experience to enhance the learning of new diabetes information.

12. You are planning an educational activity that you hope can change the learners' perceptions and values associated with health and diabetes management. Which domain of learning will you be addressing with this educational activity?

   A. The health beliefs domain
   B. The e cognitive domain
   C. The affective domain
   D. The psychological domain

13. Which teaching/learning strategy is the most appropriate when you are teaching the learners to change their perceptions and values associated with health and diabetes management?

   A. A lecture/discussion
   B. Demonstration and return demonstration
   C. Role playing
   D. Reading material

14. Which developmental task, according to Erikson, is the least likely to be achieved?

   A. Self-actualization
   B. Esteem by others
   C. Sensorimotor
   D. Abstraction

15. You are caring for an adolescent patient who has diabetes. Which developmental task is this patient striving to fulfill?

   A. Identity formation
   B. Ego integrity
   C. Generativity
   D. Trust

16. Your patient is not able to fully understand information well enough to be able to use it to make appropriate health care decisions. Which barrier to learning does this patient most likely have?

   A. Health illiteracy
   B. Lack of motivation
   C. A cognitive impairment
   D. High level stress

17. Whose model or theory is most often used to prioritize patient needs and problems?

    A. Maslow
    B. Orem
    C. Rogers
    D. Seyle

18. Freedom from a nosocomial infection is an example of what type of human need?

    A. A physical need
    B. A psychological need
    C. A safety need
    D. A physiological need

19. Random variances occur as the result of :

    A. Errors and mistakes made by the diabetes educator
    B. Patient barriers to change and learning
    C. Process defects that occur intermittently when a process is carried out
    D. Process defects that occur each time a process is carried out

20. Your elderly diabetic patient has dysphagia after a stroke. Which healthcare team members will collaborate with the patient and the diabetes educator to assess and address their needs?

    A. The speech and language and physical therapists
    B. The dietician and the occupational therapist
    C. The speech and language therapist and the occupational therapist
    D. The speech and language therapist and the dietician

21. Which stage of the decision-making process is the one that is most challenging and often not accurate?

    A. Determining alternatives
    B. Selecting the best option for action
    C. Defining the problem
    D. Evaluating the outcome of the decision

22. Your patient had an expected outcome of being able to correctly self-inject insulin and the timeframe was "within one week". The patient, after one week, is able to draw up the accurate dosage and also able to inject correctly, but the prepping of the site with alcohol is not being done correctly. What should do about this goal?

   A. Continue it because the goal was partially met and, given more time, it is realistic that the patient can completely meet it
   B. Discontinue it because the goal was not met
   C. Discontinue it because it is not a realistic goal
   D. Continue it because pre-established goals cannot be discontinued

23. What term is used to describe a set of practices, customs, beliefs and attitudes that is passed from generation to generation?

   A. Ethnicity
   B. Spirituality
   C. Culture
   D. Religion

24. An example of an innate emotional stressor is:

   A. Loss and grief.
   B. Polluted air.
   C. Contaminated water.
   D. Temperature extremes.

25. Your diabetic patient has just been diagnosed with end stage renal disease and the patient's daughter has expressed extreme sorrow about their mother and their mother's condition. What type of loss is this daughter most likely experiencing?

   A. Anticipatory loss
   B. Perceived loss
   C. Actual loss
   D. Profound loss

26. Which factor negatively influences the communication process in the diabetes educator-patient relationship?

   A. Knowing that the diabetes educator is educated and competent
   B. An environment that facilitates the patient's ventilation of feelings
   C. Viewing the diabetes educator in a position of authority
   D. Silence during a conversation on the part of the diabetes educator

27. Select the theorist who is accurately paired with a stage of change that occurs when the individual, or group, fully accepts and implements the desired change.

    A. Rogers: Freezing
    B. Rogers: Unfreezing
    C. Lewin: Freezing
    D. Lewin: Refreezing

28. The diabetes educator, as change agent, provides the patient with knowledge and information about the benefits of change, according to whose theory?

    A. Havelock
    B. Rogers
    C. Orem
    D. Lippitt

29. Which model of health and illness is most closely aligned with Hans Seyle's theory of stress?

    A. The Adaptation Model
    B. The Health-Illness Continuum
    C. The Dimensions Model
    D. The Agent – Host – Environment Model

30. Select the level of prevention that is accurately paired with its description.

    A. Quaternary prevention: The focus on the prevention of any occurrence of disease
    B. Primary prevention: Screening
    C. Tertiary prevention: Restoration of function
    D. Secondary prevention: Risk assessment

31. Select the teaching strategy that is correctly paired with the domain of learning.

    A. Discussion: Cognitive domain
    B. Demonstration: Cognitive domain
    C. Demonstration: Affective domain
    D. Discussion: Psychomotor domain

32. Educational content should be sequenced according to movement from the:

    A. Threatening to non-threatening
    B. Psychomotor to the cognitive domain
    C. Unknown to the known
    D. Simple to the complex

33. According to the Agent – Host – Environment Model of Clark and Leavell, which is an example of an agent?

   A. The diabetic patient
   B. Risk factors
   C. High glucose levels
   D. Genetic makeup

34. Dunn's model of High – Level Wellness Model describes an uncontrolled diabetic with poor nutrition who lives in a community without fresh fruits and vegetables as a patient with:

   A. Emergent wellness in an unfavorable environment
   B. Poor health in an unfavorable environment
   C. Protected poor health in an unfavorable environment
   D. Emergent poor health in an unfavorable environment

35. According to Erikson, which developmental age group is tasked with generativity, productivity, and concern about others?

   A. Middle aged adults
   B. Older adults
   C. Adolescents
   D. Young adults

36. Select the level of development that is accurately paired with its characteristics.

   A. Young Adult: Isolation
   B. Infancy: Stagnation
   C. Preschool Child: Shame and doubt
   D. School Age Child: Guilt and fear of punishment

37. Which aspect of the human being is the conscience according to Freud?

   A. The id
   B. The superego
   C. The ego
   D. The phallic stage

38. Stella Chess and Alexander Thomas developed a theory of growth and development that focuses on what?

    A. The six age groups and the physical, psychological and social tasks associated with each

    B. The seven stages of young to older adulthood

    C. The positive changes associated with the aging process.

    D. The nine temperamental qualities of young children

39. Which development task is associated with one's acceptance of one's own demise without fear, according to Peck?

    A. Body Transcendence versus Body Preoccupation

    B. Ego Differentiation versus Work Role Preoccupation

    C. Ego Transcendence versus Ego Preoccupation

    D. Spiritual Differentiation versus Work Role Preoccupation

40. Nutrition and nutritional patterns are most often affected by:

    A. Personal preferences and gourmet skills

    B. Cultural and religious practices

    C. Household cleanliness and time constraints

    D. All of the above

41. What is the alternative term for isotonic exercise?

    A. Static exercise

    B. Setting exercise

    C. Resistive exercise

    D. Dynamic exercise

42. The types of exercise can be classified according to:

    A. The type of muscle contraction

    B. The amount of muscle contraction

    C. The amount of movement required

    D. The amount of limited movement

43. Resistive exercises are also referred to as:

    A. Isometric exercise

    B. Isotonic exercise

    C. Isokinetic exercise

    D. Aerobic exercise

44. What type of exercise is also referred to as static exercise?

   A. Isotonic exercise
   B. Isokinetic exercise
   C. Isometric exercise
   D. Aerobic exercise

45. What type of exercise takes in more oxygen than is needed to perform the exercise?

   A. Isotonic
   B. Aerobic
   C. Isokinetic
   D. Anaerobic

46. When exercising, the metabolic rate is:

   A. Decreased for the time a patient is exercising
   B. Increased for the first twenty minutes of exercise
   C. Increased during the entire exercise session
   D. Increased during and even after the exercise

47. A FIT exercise program is:

   A. A plan that anyone can use
   B. A must for anyone over the age of 60
   C. An individualized tailored program
   D. A program for those who use a wheelchair

48. Actual losses:

   A. Cannot be verified by others.
   B. Can be verified by others.
   C. Are the same as perceived losses.
   D. Do not affect a person.

49. The first three phases of grieving in correct sequential order, according to Engel's theory include:

   A. Shock and disbelief, developing awareness and restitution
   B. Developing awareness, shock and renewal
   C. Developing awareness, shock and restitution
   D. Shock, awareness of the loss and conservation and withdrawal

50. Whose theory of grieving includes the unique phase of bargaining?

    A. Engel's
    B. Sander's
    C. Maslow's
    D. Kubler Ross's

51. As you are planning an educational activity with your diabetic patient, the patient states, "I just don't know if this teaching will be helpful to me because I developed diabetes because my wife has chosen and prepared fattening foods for our entire marriage. What barrier to learning does this patient demonstrate with this comment?

    A. Stress
    B. Depression
    C. An external locus of control
    D. A loss of control and motivation

52. The diabetes educator can change a patient's external locus of control by:

    A. Providing the education to the caregiver rather than the patient
    B. Eliminating all unnecessary stressors from the patient's life
    C. Being culturally sensitive and culturally competent
    D. Convincing the patient that they can control and cope with diabetes

53. One of the most effective ways to motivate diabetic learners is to:

    A. Listen and hear all of the patient's concerns and fears
    B. Have the learner actively participate in all phases of the teaching
    C. Have the caregiver actively participate in all phases of the teaching
    D. Provide a quiet and comfortable environment without distractions

54. Encouraging the learner to reflect on readings, contemplate applications and summarize material rather than the memorizing facts is an effective strategy for a diabetic patient with which type of learning style or preference?

    A. Active learning
    B. Visual learning
    C. Reflective learning
    D. Intuitive learning

55. Which learning style characterizes learners who prefer detail-oriented learning and practical, real world oriented learning rather than abstraction?

    A. Sensing learners
    B. Reflective learners
    C. Intuitive learners
    D. Verbal learners

56. When the diabetic patient states that they are "very dizzy and weak", it is an example of:

    A. Emergent data
    B. Extraneous data
    C. Terminal data
    D. Subjective data

57. Your patient's blood glucose level is 134. What type of data is this?

    A. Primary, qualitative data
    B. Primary, quantitative data
    C. Secondary, qualitative data
    D. Secondary, quantitative data

58. Which of the following is included in the patient's health history?

    A. The peripheral circulation to the lower legs
    B. The patient's life style choices, including diet
    C. The assessment of the family dynamics
    D. The assessment of the patient's glucose levels

59. Select the pharmacological term that is correctly paired with its definition.

    A. Trade or brand name: The manufacturer's name for the drug. Trade name drugs are more expensive than generic drugs
    B. Trade or brand name: The manufacturer's name for the drug. Trade name drugs are less expensive than generic drugs
    C. Excretion: The breakdown of a drug, or medication, in the liver
    D. Drug distribution: The breakdown of a drug, or medication, in the liver

60. Which commonly occurring fear among diabetic patients can be allayed with education relating to the anatomy and physiology of the skin?

    A. Needle phobia
    B. Drawing up the accurate insulin dosage
    C. Hypoglycemia
    D. Weight gain

61. A commonly occurring and verbalized fear among newly diagnosed diabetes patients is:

    A. Losses of sexual desire
    B. Losses of sexual functioning
    C. A loss of social interaction
    D. Life style changes

62. Your diabetic patient enjoys eating out and restaurants. The patient is reluctant and resistant to eliminating their dining out pleasures because of their diabetes. What should you do?

    A. Tell them that dining out has to stop in order to maintain blood glucose levels
    B. Assess their dining out patterns and choices and modify them as indicated
    C. Advise the patient that non-home prepared foods contain too much glucose
    D. Tell them that only vegetarian restaurants are safe for people with diabetes

63. The primary purpose of assessing dietary patterns among diabetic patients is to:

    A. Admonish the patient about correct dietary choices
    B. Admonish the significant other about correct dietary choices
    C. Remind them of the diabetes diet and its restrictions
    D. Determine what the patient is eating on a regular basis

64. Which of the following is NOT a risk factor associated with mental illness?

    A. Age
    B. Gender
    C. Diabetes
    D. Geography

65. Which type of mental illness most often affects patients with diabetes?

    A. A mood disorder
    B. A mixed disorder
    C. A thought disorder
    D. A behavioral disorder

66. Your patient is currently having feelings of dread and apprehension regarding their newly diagnosed diabetes and, when you check the person's pulse, it is 126/min. Which psychological impairment is the patient most likely affected with?

    A. Grief
    B. Depression
    C. Anxiety
    D. Maladaptation

67. Your patient expresses feelings of helplessness and hopelessness relating to their diabetes and diabetes control. Which psychological impairment is the patient most likely affected with?

    A. Grief
    B. Depression
    C. Anxiety
    D. Maladaptation

68. Select the developmental theorist that is correctly paired with their theory.

    A. Erikson: Hierarchy of Needs
    B. Piaget: Physical Stages of Development
    C. Freud: The Eight Age Groups of Development
    D. Havighurst: The Six Age Groups of Development

69. Your new diabetic patient is self-reflective and value driven. The patient also is aware of their own life as finite. How old is this patient most likely to be?

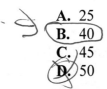

    A. 25
    B. 40
    C. 45
    D. 50

70. Which developmentalist addresses cognitive development within the context of culture?

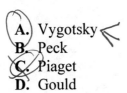

    A. Vygotsky
    B. Peck
    C. Piaget
    D. Gould

71. Which developmental theorist includes only older adults in their developmental model?

    A. Vygotsky
    B. Peck
    C. Gould
    D. Piaget

72. Which of the following is NOT considered a barrier to effective learning?

    A. Moderate stress
    B. Impaired cognition
    C. Cultural impacts
    D. Depression

73. The patient's level of motivation is determined during which phase of the teaching/learning process?

    A. Planning
    B. Implementation
    C. Assessment
    D. Evaluation

74. Which aspect of physical assessment does the diabetes educator most likely perform?

    A. Breath sounds
    B. Heart sounds
    C. Kidney functioning
    D. Injection sites

75. Select the physical assessment technique that is correctly paired with it description.

    A. Palpation: Palpation can consist of light or deep palpation
    B. Percussion: Percussion uses the sense of touch
    C. Auscultation: A visual assessment of the sense of hearing
    D. Inspection: Inspection is the second step of the assessment

76. According to the Centers for Disease Control and Prevention, your diabetic patient is considered obese when they have a BMI of:

A. 10
B. 20
C. 27
D. 35

77. Your patient weighs 75 kg and their height is 1.65 meters. What is the patient's BMI?

A. 30
B. 45
C. 50
D. 55

78. Pulses can be assessed in which bodily area?

A. The shoulder area
B. On the pinna
C. On the abdomen
D. In the groin area

79. Which vital sign is most consciously controlled?

A. Respiratory rate
B. Pulse rate
C. Blood glucose level
D. Blood pressure

80. What are the normal parameters for a fasting blood glucose level?

A. 70-100 mg/dL
B. 100-110 mg/dL
C. 100-120 mg/dL
D. 100-130 mg/dL

81. Basal insulin from an insulin pump is delivered:

A. Only at those times when the patient needs to correct high blood glucose levels
B. When the patient is eating
C. Between meals and overnight over a 24 hour period
D. Between meals and overnight over a 12 hour period

82. When an A1C test is used as a diagnostic test, which level indicates diabetes?

    A. Between 4 and 4.5
    B. Between 4.5 and 5
    C. Between 5.5 and 6
    D. 6.5 or higher

83. How many classifications of medications are used in the U.S. to manage blood glucose levels?

    A. 4
    B. 6
    C. 9
    D. 12

84. What diagnosis is appropriate when the patient's blood glucose is higher than normal but has not yet reached the criteria for the diagnosis of type 2 diabetes?

    A. Prediabetes
    B. Type 1 diabetes
    C. Gestational Diabetes
    D. Diabetes mellitus

85. The most common symptoms of diabetes mellitus are the direct result of:

    A. Diuresis
    B. Hypotension
    C. Hypoglycemia
    D. Hyperglycemia

86. What leads to three of the most commonly occurring complications of diabetes, namely, retinopathy, nephropathy and neuropathy?

    A. Cardiac arrest
    B. Arterial flutter
    C. Microvascular damage
    D. Macrovascular damage

87. Which is the most commonly occurring form of diabetic neuropathy?

    A. Radiculopathy
    B. Cranial neuropathy
    C. Symmetric polyneuropathy
    D. Autonomic neuropathy

88. What is the single most effective way to prevent nosocomial infections in our healthcare facilities?

    A. Changing open wound dressings
    B. Disinfection
    C. Sterilization
    D. Hand washing

89. Actual losses:

    A. Can be verified by others
    B. Cannot be verified by others
    C. Are also known as perceived losses
    D. Do not affect the person

90. What types of patients should be screened for falls?

    A. All patients
    B. The elderly
    C. The confused or elderly
    D. The confused elderly and mentally ill

91. What is the name of the process that is used to dig down to the deepest, real reasons why mistakes and errors have occurred?

    A. Peer review
    B. Root cause analysis
    C. Variance tracking
    D. Benchmarking

92. Which phase of the decision making process is most prone to errors?

    A. Ranking and weighing criteria
    B. Deciding on the best alternative
    C. Problem definition
    D. Implementing the course of action

93. Nosocomial infections are:

    A. Infections that a patient does not have upon admission, but gets while in a healthcare facility
    B. Infections that a patient receives at home from a household cleaning agent
    C. Infections that a patient gets chronically throughout their life
    D. Infections that are only airborne and spread through respiration and an open wound

94. What is the first phase of viral hepatitis?

    A. Induction phase
    B. Posticteric phase
    C. Preicteric phase
    D. Icteric phase

95. Dental caries are also known as:

    A. Cavities
    B. Root canals
    C. Fillings
    D. Gum recesses

96. What body parts are affected by diabetes?

    A. Skin, teeth, bones, heart and nails
    B. Skin, teeth, heart and blood vessels
    C. Skin, teeth, heart, lungs and blood vessels
    D. All

97. Which of the following appears as firm, yellow, pea-like enlargements in the skin?

    A. Eruptive xanthomatosis
    B. Diabetic blisters
    C. Necrobiosis lipoidica diabeticorum
    D. Diabetic dermopathy

98. A diabetic meal plan allows for consuming 8 oz. of what type(s) of milk?

    A. 1% and 2%
    B. Skim and 1%
    C. Skim, 1% and 2%
    D. Whole milk

99. Nephropathy is also known as:

    A. Liver damage
    B. Kidney damage
    C. Nerve damage
    D. Skin damage

100. Neuropathy is also known as:

    A. Kidney damage
    B. Liver damage
    C. Skin damage
    D. Nerve damage

101. Your newly diagnosed diabetic patient tells you that they are "now cured" of their diabetes because "my blood glucose levels are lower than normal after only 2 weeks of treatment". How should you reply to this patient comment?

    A. You are not cured. You are most likely affected with the honeymoon period
    B. You are not cured. You are most likely affected with the dawn effect
    C. You are not cured. You are most likely affected with the Somogyi effect
    D. Congratulations. I am glad that you are back to normal

102. Which of these two phenomena are most similar?

    A. The dawn effect and the dusk effect
    B. The dusk effect and the Somogyi effect
    C. The dawn effect and the Somogyi effect
    D. The honeymoon period and the Somogyi effect

103. The honeymoon effect occurs because the:

    A. The patient is successfully and effectively managing their prediabetes with diet and exercise
    B. The type 2 diabetic patient has been able to reduce their BMI and their bodily weight
    C. The digestion of carbohydrates has increased thus increasing insulin production
    D. Pancreatic islet cells produce more insulin than prior to the treatment of the diabetes

104. As you examine your diabetic patient's record keeping, you notice that the patient's 2 am blood glucose levels are low for three days in succession. What is this patient most likely affected with?

    A. Nocturnal hyperglycemia
    B. The Somogyi effect
    C. hyperosmolar nonketotic syndrome
    D. Nocturnal ketoacidosis

105. Illnesses often lead to what among diabetic patients?

    A. Hyperglycemia
    B. Hypoglycemia
    C. Ketoacidosis among type 2 diabetic patients
    D. Hyperosmolar hyperglycemic nonketotic coma among type 1 diabetic patients

106. You are developing a Sick Day plan for your patient. This patient is an adolescent with type 1 diabetes. What should be included in this plan?

    A. The need to check blood glucose levels and for urinary ketones at least every 4 hours
    B. The need to check blood glucose levels and for urinary ketones at least every 6 hours
    C. The need to check blood glucose levels and for urinary ketones at least 4 times per day
    D. The need to check blood glucose levels and for urinary ketones at least 2 times per day

107. Diabetic patients who travel must be aware of the fact they must bring an ample supply of medications and supplies and also that they should carry these things with them when boarding a plane, rather than checking them in, because:

    A. These items, like needles, must remain sterile and not contaminated
    B. Insulin and other medications cannot be subjected to pressure changes
    C. Insulin and other medications deteriorate with altitude changes on a plane
    D. These items are often lost or late when they are checked in

108. One of the normal changes of the aging process that directly impacts on diabetes management and control is:

    A. Increased metabolism
    B. Diminished metabolism
    C. Obesity
    D. Overweightness

109. Diabetes educators should provide educational activities to women with existing diabetes during childbearing years about:

    A. The need to take 5 mg of folic acid supplementation for at least 4 weeks after conception
    B. The need to take 10mg of folic acid supplementation for at least 4 weeks after conception
    C. Avoiding unplanned pregnancies

D. The need to take 10 mg of folic acid supplementation for at least 12 weeks after conception

110. The most commonly occurring complication of hypertension among diabetic patients is:

A. Renal disorders
B. Diabetic retinopathy
C. Neuropathy
D. Hyperosmolar hyperglycemic nonketotic coma

111. Your diabetic patient has celiac disease. What information about diabetes and celiac disease should your patient be knowledgeable about?

A. Celiac disease alters carbohydrate absorption
B. Celiac disease increases carbohydrate absorption
C. Celiac disease alters lactose absorption
D. Celiac disease increases lactose absorption

112. Which of the following is the most challenging in terms of diabetes management and control?

A. Fixed night shifts
B. Rotating work shifts
C. Religiously mandated fast days
D. A Romanian culture's Christmas practices

113. Your obese, newly diagnosed 76 year old female is complaining about daytime lethargy/tiredness and her spouse is complaining about her snoring. Which disorder is this patient most likely affected with?

A. Neurogenic sleep apnea
B. Nocturnal hypoglycemia
C. Nocturnal hyperglycemia
D. Obstructive sleep apnea

114. Which term is most appropriate to describe research-based practice?

A. Evidence based practice
B. Benchmarked practice
C. A best practice
D. Empirical research

115. As a certified diabetes educator, you can access research and evidence based practices at:

    A. Web MD
    B. The American Diabetes Association
    C. The Joanna Briggs Institute
    D. The National Institutes of Health

116. Jaundice results from increases of which of the following?

    A. Albumin
    B. Bilirubin
    C. Glutamic
    D. Lacatate

117. Male patients should be encouraged to eat how many grams of fiber a day?

    A. 28
    B. 32
    C. 38
    D. 46

118. Female patients should be encouraged to eat how many grams of fiber a day?

    A. 25
    B. 28
    C. 32
    D. 36

119. The percent of daily value on a food label is based on how many calories per day?

    A. 1000
    B. 1200
    C. 1500
    D. 2000

120. What color are the bags, containers or bins that are available for the safe disposal of sharps in healthcare facilities?

    A. Blue
    B. Green
    C. Red
    D. Yellow

121. The American Diabetes Association's ABCs approach to diabetes management stands for:

    A. A1C, blood glucose and cholesterol
    B. A1C, blood pressure and cholesterol
    C. A1C, blood glucose and contamination
    D. Airborne, blood borne and chemically formed

122. What condition is present when the patient has abnormal concentrations of lipids in their blood?

    A. Dyslipidemia
    B. Paresthesia
    C. Acrolipidemia
    D. Sclerodactyly

123. Which term relates to the patient's ability to sense the location, position and orientation of their body and their body parts?

    A. Capsulitis
    B. Proprioception
    C. Anisocoria
    D. Dupuytren contracture

124. When too much NPH insulin is drawn into the needle when mixing it with regular insulin, the patient should be instructed to:

    A. Eject the overage back into the vial
    B. Eject the overage into the sink
    C. Eject all of the insulin and start again
    D. Start over with a new needle

125. Glycogen is:

    A. Lipids present in the blood
    B. Lipids that are converted in the body cells
    C. Glucose that is stored in the liver and muscle
    D. Glucose that converts to lipids

126. What part of the pancreas produces insulin?

    A. Exocrine pancreas
    B. Endocrine pancreas
    C. Peripheral pancreas
    D. Threshold pancreas

127. Glucophage belongs to which classification of medication?

    A. Sulfonylureas
    B. Meglitinides
    C. Biguanides
    D. Thiazolidinediones

128. How many employees must a company have and within what mile range in order for employees to be eligible for the benefits of the Family Medical Leave Act?

    A. 50 people within 50 miles
    B. 50 people within 75 miles
    C. 75 people within 50 miles
    D. 75 people within 75 miles

129. The federal government considers whom as immediate family members under the Family Medical Leave Act?

    A. A child, spouse, parent, grandparent and sibling
    B. A child, spouse, parent and sibling
    C. A child, spouse and parent
    D. A child, spouse, domestic partner, child and parent

130. Caffeine is a stimulant that can result in:

    A. High blood pressure
    B. Low blood pressure
    C. High blood glucose levels
    D. Low blood glucose levels

131. Polyols are:

    A. A drooping eyelid
    B. Starches
    C. Sugar alcohol
    D. Unsaturated fats

132. Good fats include:

    A. Polyunsaturated and saturated
    B. Saturated and monounsaturated
    C. Polyunsaturated and trans fats
    D. Monounsaturated and polyunsaturated

133. Unhealthy fats include:

    A. Saturated and monounsaturated
    B. Monounsaturated and trans fats
    C. Trans fats and monounsaturated
    D. Saturated and trans fats

134. When a patient exercises more than usual:

    A. They do not use enough glucose
    B. They use up more glucose than usual
    C. They are at risk for high blood glucose levels
    D. They usually sweat less than normal

135. What is the term that refers to an unequal pupil size?

    A. Diplopia
    B. Anisocoria
    C. Trochlear
    D. Macrovascular disease

136. Diabetes management plans are:

    A. Prepared according to age
    B. Prepared according to type of diabetes
    C. Prepared according to the gender of the patient
    D. Prepared specifically for each individual patient

137. Without prior written consent a patient's medical information:

    A. Can only be shared with family members
    B. Can only be shared with the patient's spouse or domestic partner
    C. Can only be shared with those who are providing direct medical care to the patient
    D. Cannot be shared with anyone

138. Which decision making process respects the patient and their opinion?

    A. Paternalistic
    B. Maternalistic
    C. Patient sovereignty
    D. Shared decision making

139. The CDE shall provide services based on:

    A. High payment scales
    B. Their personal interest in a case
    C. Patient needs and not solely for personal financial gain
    D. What patients are more interesting than others

140. Job descriptions and job functions are determined by:

    A. Employing agencies
    B. The CDE credential
    C. The grades on the CDE exam
    D. State practice acts

ANSWER KEY

1. Answer: B	49. Answer: A	97. Answer: A
2. Answer: A	50. Answer: D	98. Answer: B
3. Answer: D	51. Answer: C	99. Answer: B
4. Answer: D	52. Answer: D	100. Answer: D
5. Answer: B	53. Answer: B	101. Answer: A
6. Answer: C	54. Answer: C	102. Answer: C
7. Answer: A	55. Answer: A	103. Answer: D
8. Answer: C	56. Answer: D	104. Answer: B
9. Answer: B	57. Answer: D	105. Answer: A
10. Answer: D	58. Answer: B	106. Answer: A
11. Answer: A	59. Answer: A	107. Answer: D
12. Answer: C	60. Answer: A	108. Answer: B
13. Answer: C	61. Answer: D	109. Answer: C
14. Answer: A	62. Answer: B	110. Answer: A
15. Answer: A	63. Answer: D	111. Answer: A
16. Answer: A	64. Answer: D	112. Answer: B
17. Answer: A	65. Answer: A	113. Answer: D
18. Answer: C	66. Answer: C	114. Answer: A
19. Answer: D	67. Answer: B	115. Answer: C
20. Answer: D	68. Answer: D	116. Answer: B
21. Answer: C	69. Answer: B	117. Answer: C
22. Answer: A	70. Answer: A	118. Answer: A
23. Answer: C	71. Answer: B	119. Answer: D
24. Answer: A	72. Answer: A	120. Answer: C
25. Answer: A	73. Answer: C	121. Answer: B
26. Answer: C	74. Answer: D	122. Answer: A
27. Answer: D	75. Answer: A	123. Answer: B
28. Answer: B	76. Answer: D	124. Answer: D
29. Answer: A	77. Answer: B	125. Answer: C
30. Answer: C	78. Answer: D	126. Answer: B
31. Answer: A	79. Answer: A	127. Answer: C
32. Answer: D	80. Answer: A	128. Answer: B
33. Answer: C	81. Answer: C	129. Answer: C
34. Answer: B	82. Answer: D	130. Answer: A
35. Answer: A	83. Answer: B	131. Answer: C
36. Answer: A	84. Answer: A	132. Answer: D
37. Answer: B	85. Answer: D	133. Answer: D
38. Answer: D	86. Answer: C	134. Answer: B
39. Answer: C	87. Answer: C	135. Answer: B
40. Answer: B	88. Answer: D	136. Answer: D
41. Answer: D	89. Answer: A	137. Answer: C
42. Answer: A	90. Answer: A	138. Answer: D
43. Answer: C	91. Answer: B	139. Answer: C
44. Answer: C	92. Answer: C	140. Answer: A
45. Answer: B	93. Answer: A	
46. Answer: D	94. Answer: C	
47. Answer: C	95. Answer: A	
48. Answer: B	96. Answer: D	

FREE DVD **FREE** **FREE DVD**

Certified Diabetes Educator Exam Essential Test Tips DVD from Trivium Test Prep!

Dear Customer,

Thank you for purchasing from Trivium Test Prep! We're honored to help you prepare for your Certified Diabetes Educator Exam.

To show our appreciation, we're offering a **FREE *Certified Diabetes Educator Exam Essential Test Tips* DVD by Trivium Test Prep**. Our DVD includes 35 test preparation strategies that will make you successful on the Certified Diabetes Educator Exam. All we ask is that you email us your feedback and describe your experience with our product. Amazing, awful, or just so-so: we want to hear what you have to say!

To receive your **FREE *Certified Diabetes Educator Exam Essential Test Tips* DVD**, please email us at 5star@triviumtestprep.com. Include "Free 5 Star" in the subject line and the following information in your email:

1. The title of the product you purchased.
2. Your rating from 1 – 5 (with 5 being the best).
3. Your feedback about the product, including how our materials helped you meet your goals and ways in which we can improve our products.
4. Your full name and shipping address so we can send your FREE *Certified Diabetes Educator Exam Essential Test Tips* DVD.

If you have any questions or concerns please feel free to contact us directly at 5star@triviumtestprep.com. Thank you!

- **Trivium Test Prep Team**

CPSIA information can be obtained
at www.ICGtesting.com
Printed in the USA
LVOW09s0349040518

575947LV00038BA/524/P

9 781635 308105